Philosophy of Science

Mel Thompson

TEACH YOURSELF BOOKS

For UK order queries: please contact Bookpoint Ltd, 78 Milton Park, Abingdon, Oxon OX14 4TD. Telephone: (44) 01235 400414, Fax: (44) 01235 400454. Lines are open from 9.00–6.00, Monday to Saturday, with a 24 hour message answering service. Email address: orders@bookpoint.co.uk

For USA order queries: please contact McGraw-Hill Customer Services, P.O. Box 545, Blacklick, OH 43004-0545, USA. Telephone 1-800-722-4726, Fax: 1-614-755-5645.
For Canada order queries: please contact McGraw-Hill Ryerson Ltd, 300 Water St, Whitby, Ontario L1N 9B6, Canada. Telephone 905 430 5000, Fax: 905 430 5020.

Long renowned as the authoritative source for self-guided learning – with more than 30 million copies sold worldwide – the *Teach Yourself* series includes over 200 titles in the fields of languages, crafts, hobbies, business and education.

British Library Cataloguing in Publication Data
A catalogue record for this title is available from The British Library.

Library of Congress Catalog Card Number: On file

First published in UK 2001 by Hodder Headline Plc, 338 Euston Road, London, NW1 3BH.

First published in US 2001 by Contemporary Books, A Division of The McGraw-Hill Companies, 4255 West Touhy Avenue, Lincolnwood (Chicago), Illinois 60712–1975 USA.

Typeset by Transet Limited, Coventry, England.
Printed in Great Britain for Hodder & Stoughton Educational, a division of Hodder Headline Plc, 338 Euston Road, London NW1 3BH by Cox & Wyman Ltd, Reading, Berkshire.

Impression number	10 9 8 7 6 5 4 3 2 1
Year	2006 2005 2004 2003 2002 2001

CONTENTS

INTRODUCTION

Over the last 400 years, science has transformed human life and society. Most of what we take for granted in terms of lifestyle – including communication, health and transport – is unthinkable without science. Even when we find that technology has created personal or environmental problems, we tend to turn to science for a remedy. If car exhausts pollute the atmosphere, we look to science to provide cleaner fuels or more efficient engines. Science is a massive problem-solving and information-providing enterprise and, generally, people have great respect for what science has achieved. But what does it mean to say that something is 'scientific'? How can one tell valid science from bogus? On what basis can we assess what scientists tell us? How do we know if what we are being told is an absolute truth or merely some temporary theory, adequate for now but soon to be replaced? What is scientific language?

These are just a few of the questions with which the philosophy of science is concerned; many more will come to light as we start to look at the way in which it works and how it relates to the research projects carried out by scientists.

Science traditionally deals with facts, with information about the world in which we live, gained as hard evidence by means of experiment and analysis. Indeed, the word 'science' comes from the Latin *scientia*, meaning 'knowledge' – so science should offer us certain knowledge, as opposed to mere opinion. But it is not that simple and we know that the process of gaining scientific knowledge is one in which the straightforward claim to deal with facts needs to be qualified, both on account of the way we reason from evidence to the framing of scientific theories, and also from the nature of the experiments on which science is based.

Many argue that scientific theories cannot be conclusively proved, but must be examined in terms of degrees of probability. But if that is so, what is the basis of all the knowledge that science has built up over the last 400 years? What about the technology on which our society is based? Surely, if something works, it must be correct!

How can we challenge the basis of scientific knowledge, when all around us is evidence for the success of the scientific enterprise? We need to examine these and other questions, by looking at the process by which science goes about its business.

The 17th and 18th centuries, which saw the rise of modern science, were a time of optimism and science was seen in the context of human progress. Reason was seen as the tool by which humankind would be emancipated from the narrowness of superstition and tradition. The experimental method of the newly developing sciences was a sign of a new commitment to harness reason for the good of humanity. There was a fundamental trust in the human ability to understand and to benefit from that understanding.

Knowledge, for science, is *proven* knowledge. In other words, it must be justified by evidence and reason. Nothing is accepted as true unless it is proved to be so or there are good reasons why it may one day be proved to be so. This determination went back, in philosophical terms, to Descartes, who refused to accept anything that he could not know for certain to be true. Of course, Descartes was aware that his senses frequently misled him and he was therefore sceptical about the raw evidence they gave him.

Although the senses do provide raw data for science, we shall be looking at the way in which science has always devised ways of trying to ensure that our senses are not deceived. In particular, by devising experiments which control nature in such a way that a single feature of it can be checked out, without being too influenced by everything else. Perhaps, during the 20th century, something of that optimism was lost, understandably so. The benefits of science and technology were clear for anyone to see and yet Europe had been plunged into conflicts and had witnessed barbarity equalling anything from the previously ‘unenlightened’ ages. Science was seen as a tool that could bring benefits, but also as a curse, giving misguided humanity the ability to wage war on a scale previously unimaginable and to devastate the environment. Hence, from those campaigning against nuclear weapons during the cold war or currently campaigning against the use of genetically modified crops, there is the fear that science is dangerous and easily misused.

For much of the time, the philosophy of science examines the principles by which scientists examine evidence and frame hypotheses and the way in which science as a whole makes progress. In other words, it looks at the internal, logical workings of scientific enterprise. But beyond that, it is important to consider the implications of science as a whole for human self-understanding – in other words, to examine what part science plays in our theory of knowledge (epistemology) and the impact it has in some areas of ethics.

Natural philosophy

Until the 18th century, science and philosophy were not regarded as separate disciplines. Natural philosophy was the term used for the branch of philosophy that sought to understand the fundamental structure and nature of the universe, whether by theoretical or experimental methods.

With the development of 'modern' science through the 18th and 19th centuries, however, there developed a range of specialist interests and methodologies, so that particular scientific experimentation and observation started to separate off from the more general and theoretical considerations of philosophy. It also became increasingly difficult for any one person to have a specialist working knowledge of all branches of science, quite apart from all branches of philosophy. Hence the activity of scientists and philosophers started to be distinguished, with the latter carrying out a secondary function of checking on the underlying principles of those engaged in science.

The philosophy of science, as a separate branch of philosophy, is first found in the writings of William Whewell (1794–1886), who wrote both on the history of science and also (in 1840) on *The Philosophy of the Inductive Sciences, Founded upon their History*. Nevertheless, we need to be aware that some of the greatest names in philosophy, both before and after science appeared as a separate discipline, were also involved with mathematics and science:

- It was Aristotle who set out the different sciences and gave both science and philosophy much of its later terminology.
- Descartes, Leibniz, Pascal and Russell were all mathematicians. It need hardly be said that science could have made little progress without mathematics, and mathematics is quite fundamental to logic and therefore to philosophy. In their famous book *Principia Mathematica* (1910–1913) Bertrand Russell and Alfred North Whitehead argued that mathematics was a development of deductive logic. Thus much of what is done in science, however specialist in its application, is actually based on fundamental logical principles.
- For some, science was an influence on their overall philosophy and view of the world. Bacon, Locke and others wanted to give the scientific method a sound philosophical basis. Hume, in assessing the evidence of the senses as the basis of knowledge, was both influenced and challenged by scientific method. Hobbes saw the whole world as matter in motion – a view to be developed with mathematical precision in Newtonian physics.
- Even the philosopher Kant, who is generally seen as a writer of abstract and highly conceptual philosophy, wrote *A General Natural History and Theory of the Heavens* in 1755, in which he explored the possible origin of the solar system. His distinction between the things we observe (phenomena) and things as they are in themselves (noumena) is of fundamental importance for understanding the philosophy of science and especially for defining the relationship between the experiences one has and the actual reality which gives rise to such experiences.

But it would be wrong to think that the influence has all been one way, with philosophy gently guarding and nurturing its young, scientific offshoot. Some movements in philosophy (e.g. the logical positivists of the early 20th century) were particularly espoused by those who were qualified in the sciences and their aim, that the meaning of statements should be backed up by evidence, reflects the scientific approach.

Science cannot, of course, understand or communicate anything without using language and concepts. Hence it is a valid exercise for anyone, whether coming from a philosophical or scientific background, to explore the meaning of the language scientists use and the methodologies that govern their work.

The role of the philosophy of science

Generally speaking, the philosophy of science is that branch of philosophy that examines the methods used by science (e.g. the ways in which hypotheses and laws are formulated from evidence) and the grounds on which scientific claims about the world may be justified. Whereas scientists tend to become more and more specialised in their interests, philosophers generally stand back from the details of particular research programmes and concentrate on making sense of the overall principles and establishing how they relate together to give an overall view of the world.

Whereas science describes reality, scientism is the view that the scientific description of reality is the *only* truth there is. With the advance of science, there has been a tendency to slip into scientism and assume that any claim can be authenticated if the term 'scientific' is used to describe it. Equally, those methods of dealing with reality that are not scientific (and that includes all the arts and personal emotional and value-laden ways of encountering the world) may become labelled as 'only' subjective, and therefore of little account in terms of describing the way the world is. The essential thing for the philosophy of science, therefore, is to avoid crude scientism and to get a balanced view on what the scientific process can and cannot achieve.

The key feature of much philosophy of science concerns the nature of scientific theories – how it is that we can move from observation of natural phenomena to producing general statements about the world. And, of course, the crucial questions here concern the criteria by which one can say that a theory is correct, how one can judge between different theories that purport to explain the same phenomenon and how theories develop and change as science progresses.

And once we start to look at theories, we are dealing with all the usual philosophical problems of language and what and how we can know that something is the case. Thus philosophy of science relates to other major areas of philosophy: metaphysics (the structures of reality), epistemology (the theory of knowledge) and language (in order to explore the nature of scientific claims and the logic by which they are formulated). In doing this, it is intended that the philosophy of science should not act as some kind of intellectual policeman, but should play an active part in assisting science by clarifying the implications of its practice.

There are at least three different ways in which we can think of the relationship between philosophy and science:

- Science and philosophy can be seen as dealing with different subject matter. Science gives information about the world; philosophy deals with norms, values and meanings. Philosophy can clarify the language science uses to make its claims, can check the logic by which those claims are justified and can explore the implications of the scientific enterprise. This has been a widely held view and it gives philosophy and science very different roles.
- It can be argued that you cannot draw a clear distinction between statements about fact ('synthetic' statements, about which science has its say) and statements about meaning ('analytic' statements, which philosophy can show to be true by definition).

  Statements about meaning may often be reduced to the 'naming' of things and do not make sense without some reference to the external world. So, philosophy may be an extension of the scientific approach, dealing with questions about reality based on the findings of science. Science is full of concepts and these may be revised or explained in different ways. Science is not simply the reporting of facts, but the arguing out of theories; hence we should not expect to draw a clear line between science and philosophy. (This view was developed by the modern American philosopher W. V. Quine in an important article, published in 1951, entitled 'The two dogmas of empiricism'.

- Philosophy can describe reality, and can come to non-scientific truths about the way the world is. These truths do not depend on science, but are equally valid. (This reflects an approach taken by philosophers who are particularly concerned with the nature of language and how it relates to experience and empirical data, including Moore, Wittgenstein, Austin, Strawson and Searle.)

The key questions here are:

1. Are there aspects of reality with which science cannot deal, but philosophy can?
2. If philosophy and science deal with the same subject matter, in what way does philosophy add to what science is able to tell us?

And then, of course, one could go on to ask if you can actually do science without having some sort of philosophy. Is physics possible without metaphysics of some sort or language or logic or all the concepts and presuppositions of the language that the scientist uses to explain what he or she finds?

We shall see later that science can never be absolutely 'pure'. It can never claim to be totally free from the influences of thought, language and culture within which it takes place. In fact, science cannot even be free from economic and political structures. If a scientist wants funding for his or her research, it is necessary to show that it has some value, that it is in response to some need or that it may potentially give economic benefit. So the philosophy of science needs to be aware of, and point to, those influences. Scientific evidence or theories are seldom unambiguous; and those who fund research do so with specific questions and goals in mind, goals that cannot but influence the way in which that research is conducted.

But apart from all this, there is the more general function of philosophy, which is to analyse and clarify concepts, to examine ways of argument and to show the presuppositions, logic and validity of arguments. This is what philosophy does within any sphere – whether we are considering the philosophy of mind, religion or language. The main point of issue is whether philosophy also contributes directly to the knowledge of reality. For some time, during the middle years of the 20th century, it was assumed that the principal – indeed the only – role of philosophy was clarification. Since then there has been a broadening out of its function. You may want to consider, as various arguments are presented in this book, whether philosophy has contributed directly to human knowledge or simply clarified and systematized knowledge that has its source in scientific research or common human experience.

What this book examines

Clearly, there is a huge literature on the philosophy of science, and even more on the findings of science itself and on its history. This book claims to do no more than touch on some of the key issues, in order to give an overall perspective on what the philosophy of science is about.

- Since one cannot appreciate what science does without some overall sense of what it has done to date, we start with a brief overview of the history of science in the West. Of particular interest here are the assumptions made by scientists, and also the social implications of science and technology. The impact of science is so great that it is quite difficult to stand back and get its achievements into perspective, but that is the aim of the opening chapter.
- Science is generally defined by its method. We shall therefore examine this, particularly in the context of the rise of modern science from the 17th century.
- Science develops theories and the debate about how these are validated or refuted and replaced is a central concern for the philosophy of science. We shall therefore examine the status of scientific claims.
- But does science deal with real things in the outside world, rather than the experience we have of them or the language we use to describe them? We shall look at the claims concerning scientific realism.
- It has long been recognised that our observations are

influenced by our theories and that we may judge scientific theories by criteria other than their inherent truth. Are they useful in predicting things we need to know? Are they relevant? Can you accept two apparently contradictory theories at the same time? Relativism and relevance are key questions to explore here.

Some areas of scientific work are of particular interest:

- Chaos theory, complexity theory, issues concerning predictability and probability, whether everything is in fact determined or happens by chance, whether chance may be loaded to produce a particular result: these form a fascinating area of study, moving far from the apparent simplicity of the science of earlier centuries.
- Science has much to say about human beings, from the genetic basis of life and the social and psychological theories that seek to explain behaviour, to the possibility of creating artificial intelligence. We shall therefore look at issues related to science and humankind and also at the genetic basis of all life.
- The scientific quest has never been limited to this planet. Astronomy was an important feature of the rise of modern science and today the theories about the origins and shape of the universe, with the quest for a theory of everything, is a fascinating area of science and one which raises questions about what we can know and *how* we can know it.
- Finally, we take a look at the issues of science and authority. How does the scientific community set about assessing new ideas? What authority does scientific evidence have within society as a whole? We attempt to get the process by which science makes progress into perspective and set it within its overall social, political and economic context.

But there is more to life than science, so we may need to look at the limits of what science can offer and how it relates to other features of human life, such as art, literature, religion and the quest for self-expression and personal meaning.

1 THE HISTORY OF SCIENCE

Although the philosophy of science and the history of science are quite separate, it is difficult to see how one could appreciate the former without some knowledge of the latter. There are two key reasons for this:

1 Advances made in science reflect the underlying understanding of reality of the time in which they are made and, at the same time, help to shape that reality. Since philosophy is concerned with the most general questions about human understanding, it is natural to explore the way in which philosophy and science influence one another in an historical context.
2 In order to understand the principles that operate within science, one must know something of the way in which scientists go about their work and that in turn can be appreciated in terms of the development of science – for scientists generally respond to situations where a previously accepted theory is found to be wanting and seek to refine or replace it. Thus, the process of scientific development is illustrated by the history of science.

It is also useful, in order to get the issues that face the philosophy of science into perspective, to have a brief overview of the way in which thinking about the natural world has changed in the West over the last 2,500 years.

There have been two very major changes in perspective. The first of these took place as the world-view initiated by the Ancient Greeks (especially Aristotle) gave way to what was to become the world of Newtonian physics in what we generally see as 'the rise of modern science'. The second took place as that Newtonian view gave way to the expanding horizons in physics, brought about by relativity, quantum theory and the impact of genetics on biology, so that, by the end of the 20th century, the world of science was as different from that of the 19th century as the Newtonian world was from the ideas of the Ancient Greeks or mediaevals.

Early Greek thinkers

Ancient Greek philosophy is dominated by the work of Socrates, Plato and Aristotle, but before them was a group of thinkers generally known as the 'pre-Socratics', who developed theories to explain the nature of things, based on their observation of the natural world; they were, in effect, the first Western scientists.

Pre-Socratic thinkers

Thales (6th century BCE), who is generally regarded as the first philosopher and scientist, considered different substances, solid or liquid and came to the view (extraordinary for the 6th century BCE) that they were all ultimately reducible to a single element. He mistakenly thought that this fundamental element was water. His answer may have been wrong, but it must have taken a fantastic leap of intellect and intuition to ask that sort of question for the very first time.

Comment

Only one oxygen atom separates Thales from modern physics, for we now consider all substances ultimately to be derived from hydrogen.

From the same century, another thinker anticipated later scientific thought. **Heraclitus** argued that everything is in a state of flux and that even those things that appear to be permanent are in fact subject to a process of change. Our concepts 'river' or 'tree' may remain constant, but any actual river or tree is never static. He is best known for the expression: 'You cannot step into the same river twice.'

We live now in a world where most people take it for granted that everything from galaxies, stars and species to the cells that make up our bodies are in a constant process of change and development. But Heraclitus came to this view by observation and logic, while those around him saw the created order as static.

Leucippus and **Democritus** (from the 5th century BCE) developed the theory (**atomism**) that all matter was comprised of very small particles separated by empty space. If substances had different characteristics, it was because they were composed of different mixtures of atoms.

Notice the logic used by these early thinkers. They saw that a substance can take on different forms – solid, liquid or gas, depending on temperature (as when water boils or freezes) – and came to the general principle that the same atoms combine differently at different temperatures. In observing the world, looking for explanations for what they saw and moving from these to formulate general theories, these early philosophers were doing what we today recognize as science. They had intuition in plenty; what they lacked was any systematic or experimental method.

Plato

Whereas the 'pre-Socratics' were happy to study and theorize about the world of experience, there was another side to Greek thought that looked away from immediate experience to contemplate ideals. This is traced back to Plato, who argued that the things we see and experience around us are merely copies of eternal but unseen realities. I only know that this creature before me is a dog, because I have an intuition of 'dogginess' in general.

Therefore, in order to understand the world, a person has to look beyond the particular things that can be experienced, to an eternal realm of 'forms'. In his famous analogy of the cave (in *The Republic*), most people see no more than fleeting images, shadows cast upon the back wall of a cave by an unseen fire. Only the philosopher turns to see beyond the fire, to objects themselves, and then, up through the mouth of the cave, to the light of the sun. Reality is thus understood only by turning away from the wall and its shadows – in other words the ordinary world of our experience – and contemplating general principles and concepts.

Comment

This view, which has been immensely influential in Western thought, tends to separate off the mind from the physical world of experience. It looks outside the world for its reason and its meaning, so that the things we see have less interest for us than do the theories we have of them. This was radically different from the ideas of the pre-Socratics and it marked the point at which, much later, philosophy and science would start to move apart – with philosophy heading in the direction of language and pure ideas and science continuing to focus on the experience of the physical world and the attempt to make sense of it.

Aristotle

Aristotle (384–322BCE) argued that knowledge of the world comes through experience interpreted by reason; you need to examine **phenomena**, not turn away from them. The process of scientific thinking therefore owes more to Aristotle than to Plato. He saw knowledge as something that develops out of our structured perception and experience, bringing together all the information that comes to us from our senses. This is a key feature of the philosophy of science.

Aristotle set out the different branches of science and divided up living things into their various species and genera – a process of classification that became a major feature of science. He also established ideas of space, time and causality.

Most significantly, Aristotle argued that a thing had four different causes:

1. Its *material cause* is the physical substance out of which it is made.
2. Its *formal cause* is its nature, shape or design – that which distinguishes a statue from the material block of marble from which it has been sculpted.
3. Its *efficient cause* is that which brought it about – our usual sense of the word 'cause'.
4. Its *final cause* is its purpose or intention.

For Aristotle, all four causes were needed for a full description of an object. It was not enough to say how it worked and what it was made of, but one needed also to give it some purpose or meaning – not just 'What is it?' or 'What is it like?' but also 'What brought it about?' and 'What is it for?'.

For Aristotle, everything had a potential and a goal: its 'final cause'. Broadly, this implied that things had a purpose, related to the future, rather than being totally defined by the efficient causes that brought them about in the first place.

There are two important things to recognize in terms of Aristotle and the development of science. First, his authority was such that it was very difficult to challenge his views, as we see happening later in connection with the work of Copernicus and Galileo. But second, the development of modern science, from about the 17th century onwards, was based on a view of the nature of reality in which efficient causation dominated over final causation. In other words, the Aristotelian world where things happened in order to achieve a goal was replaced by one in which they happened because they were part of a mechanism that determined their every move. This is something of a caricature (both of Aristotle and of 17th-century science), but the shift is clear and very important for the philosophy of science.

Archimedes

All the Ancient Greeks considered so far are best known as philosophers rather than scientists (although the distinction cannot really be made, since what we call science was **natural philosophy** rather than being seen as a separate discipline). There is one person who stands out from them as probably the greatest scientist before the advent of modern science and the work of Isaac Newton; that person is **Archimedes** (287–213 BCE).

He is perhaps best known for his bath, from which he leapt shouting 'Eureka! Eureka!'. But let us reflect on the degree of sophistication of his answer to the problem set. His task was to find if a crown was made of pure gold or if it had been debased. Its weight was equal to the gold supplied. He therefore wanted to measure its volume and check it against the volume of gold of the same weight, but clearly he could not take the crown apart or melt it down in order to do so. By observing how water was displaced as he got into his bath, he had a simple method of measuring volume – by measuring the volume of water displaced when the crown was immersed in a container full of water. He checked it against the displacement produced by an equal weight of gold, found that its volume was greater and therefore concluded that a lighter metal had been added.

Notice what is involved in solving this problem. He has to recognize that the density of a pure substance is the same wherever it is found and that any introduction of a lighter material will change the overall density. He knows that density is proportional to weight and volume. He knows the weight; therefore all he needs is to check the volume. The displacement of water provides a practical answer to that task. It was a remarkable achievement for Archimedes; but not for the goldsmith, who was executed!

Another aspect of Archimedes' work is summed up in his well-known saying that given a lever and a secure place upon which to rest it, he could move the world. This referred to his work with levers, cranes and pulleys; much of which was developed for military purposes. He produced catapults and devices for grappling and hauling ships out of the water. He even used lenses to focus the Sun's rays on the besieging Roman ships, causing fires.

But his practical technologies were based on sound physical and mathematical theories.

SUMMARY

Whereas the pre-Socratics had speculated about the fundamental nature of things and Aristotle had developed key concepts and systematized the sciences, it is Archimedes who stands out as the practical scientist, using experiment and theory to solve practical problems.

The mediaeval view

The rise of modern science in the 17th and 18th centuries is often contrasted with the mediaeval world that preceded it. The caricature is that the mediaeval world was one based on authority and religion, whereas, from the 17th century all was based on evidence and reason. However, it would be a mistake to underestimate the way in which mediaeval thinking, and the universities that developed and disseminated it, made later science possible. Therefore, before turning to the rise of modern science, we need to be aware of some basic features of the thinking that went on before it and against a background of which its ideas were developed.

After Aristotle

After Aristotle, there came the ideas of the Stoics (in which the universe was designed by the *logos*, word or reason) and the Epicureans (who took a more impersonal, atomist view).

Christian theology developed against a background of the Greek ideas of the Hellenistic world. As a result, the attitude to the physical world, expressed by Christian thinkers such as St Augustine, tended towards the Platonic view that what happened on earth was but a pale reflection of the perfection of heaven.

This was reinforced by the view of the universe expounded in the 2nd century CE by **Ptolemy of Alexandria**. In this cosmology, the Earth was surrounded by ten glassy spheres on which were fixed the Sun, Moon, stars and planets. The outermost of these was regarded as the abode of God. Each sphere was thought to influence events on the Earth, which led to an interest in astrology. Everything in the spheres above the Moon was perfect and unchanging, everything below it was imperfect and constantly open to influence and change.

Greek thought was lost to the West during what are generally known as the 'dark ages', but Aristotle and other thinkers had already been translated into Arabic and were preserved, and philosophy developed, along with mathematics, by a succession of Muslim thinkers. In the 13th century, particularly as a result of the translation into Latin of Averroes' commentaries on Aristotle, this led to a reintroduction of Aristotelian thought to the West, which then spread through the newly developing network of universities.

The mediaeval synthesis

There was an amazing flowering of philosophy in the 13th century, with thinkers such as **Thomas Aquinas** (1225–1274), **Duns Scotus** (1266–1308) and **William of Ockham** (*c*.1285–1349). Universities were established throughout Europe and the 'natural philosophy' taught in them (largely based on the rediscovered works of Aristotle) was an important preparation for later developments in both philosophy and science.

Certain features of Greek (particularly Aristotelian) thought influenced the way mediaeval thinkers looked at the world around them. All physical things were thought to be made up of four elements: earth, water, air and fire. Each element had its own natural level, to which it sought to move, so for example the natural tendency for earth was to sink, water to flow down and fire to rise up, thus explaining motion.

The heavens were perfect and therefore all motion in heaven had to be perfectly circular. There was no scope for any irregularities within the heavenly spheres. This belief caused terrible problems when it came to observing the orbits of the planets and their retrograde motion – somehow, what was observed had to be resolved in terms of perfect circles. It also proved problematic for Harvey's claim that blood was pumped around the body by the heart. Such circular movement of blood was deemed inappropriate for creatures on Earth! Although mediaeval thinkers were logical, they used deductive logic. In other words, they started with principles and theories (e.g. the heavenly spheres are the realm of perfection; perfect and eternal motion is circular) and then deduced what observations ought to follow. This was in stark contrast to **inductive** arguments, as used by later science, where evidence is gathered as the basis for framing a theory.

The synthesis at which mediaeval theologians like Aquinas worked was one in which the basic teachings of Christianity were to be wedded to the overall metaphysics of Aristotle. The result was, in its day, both intellectually and emotionally satisfying; combining the best in philosophy with a religious outlook that gave full expression to Aristotle's 'final causation' – in other words, that everything had a purpose.

When the mediaeval person looked up to the stars and planets, set in fixed crystalline spheres, he or she saw meaning and significance, because the Earth was at the centre of the universe and the life of mankind was the special object of God's concern. A rational universe, established by an 'unmoved mover', protects the human mind against the despair and nihilism of a world where everything is a product of chance. It offers an intellectual structure in which human life has purpose and meaning. A synthesis of that sort was not one to be given up lightly.

This is not to deny that, at a popular level, life in mediaeval times was full of irrational beliefs and superstitions. But the arguments between those who held traditional beliefs that were steeped in this mediaeval synthesis and those who were presenting what became modern science were not all one-sided. It was not superstition verses reason, but the effort to break out of the structures of Aristotelian philosophy, whose very success had led to the assumption that it was infallible.

Note

The advances of the 16th and 17th centuries were therefore made against a background of an established and authoritative philosophy, largely based on Aristotle. It was the need to find a new basis for knowledge that led thinkers (e.g. Francis Bacon) to define the principles of scientific method and the interpretation of evidence, distinguishing that method from the acceptance of views on the basis of authority and deductive logic.

Aristotle had always emphasized the importance of evidence, and yet the authority given to his conclusions could sometimes be given priority over new evidence. Thus **Copernicus** (1473–1543), who considered the Sun rather than the Earth to be at the centre of the known universe (see page 13) and later Galileo (1564–1642), who compared the Copernican view with that of Aristotle and Ptolemy, both sheltered their radical views from criticism by claiming that the new view of the cosmos was chiefly to be used as a theoretical model for simplifying calculations, rather than as a picture of what was actually the case. In later departing from this position, Galileo was seen to be attacking the authority of the traditional Ptolemaic view, which appeared to be confirmed by the Bible.

However, the mediaeval world was certainly not devoid of imaginative thinkers prepared to explore science and technology in a way that was free from the weight of traditional thinking. **Roger Bacon** (1220–1292), based his work on observation and was highly critical of the tendency to accept something as true simply on the grounds of authority. Among many other things, he set down ideas for developing flying machines and his work on optics led to the invention of the magnifying glass and spectacles.

Leonardo da Vinci (1452–1519) was an amazingly imaginative engineer and visionary, as well as a stunning artist and experienced architect. His ability to observe nature carefully and to consider the possible application that those observed mechanisms might have is evident in his notebooks. Like Bacon, he was fascinated by the idea of flying and had notions of planes, helicopters and parachutes.

Generally speaking, mediaeval thought, following the influence of Aristotle (whose work was taught in universities throughout Europe from about 1250), was based on looking at essences and potentials. Knowing the essence of something revealed its final purpose and achieving that purpose was to turn its potentiality into actuality. The world was not seen as a random collection of atoms or as an impersonal machine, but as the environment where each thing, with its own particular essence, could seek its final purpose and fulfilment. The final purpose of the baby was the adult into which it would grow. With such a philosophy, the task of one who examines natural things is not physical analysis, but the discovery of essence and purpose. With hindsight, that looks like a religious interpretation of the world, but in fact it was simply the outcome of a philosophy that took seriously Aristotle's idea of 'final' causes.

The rise of modern science

With the Renaissance and the Reformation, there emerged in Europe a general appreciation of the value of human reason and its ability to challenge established ideas. Scepticism was widespread. The 17th century witnessed political debate at every level of society, as we see in the Civil War in England and its aftermath. The rise of science should therefore be seen against a cultural background of new ideas, of individual liberty and of the overthrow of traditional authority, both political and religious.

Francis Bacon (1561–1626) initiated what was to become the norm of scientific method, by insisting that all knowledge should be based on evidence and experiment. In doing this, he rejected Aristotle's idea that everything had a final cause or purpose. Rather than observing nature with preconceived notions about what should be found, he started with the observation of individual things, and from them reasoned towards general principles. He famously warned about 'idols' that stood in the way of knowledge, including:

- the wish to accept whatever evidence seems to confirm what we already believe
- the distortion that results from our habitual ways of thinking
- muddles that come from a careless use of language
- accepting the authority of a particular person or group.

He also argued that, in gathering evidence, one should not simply try to find cases to confirm one's expectations, but should consider contrary examples as well. In this, he anticipated the work of the 20th-century philosopher Karl Popper, who made falsification the key to progress in science.

In other words

You can't claim that a theory is based on evidence and then pick and choose which evidence you accept, depending on whether or not it fits the theory! The crucial test of a theory comes when you find a piece of evidence that goes against it. Then you know that something is wrong with the way you gathered that evidence, or else that the theory needs to be modified.

Overall, it is important to recognize that Bacon saw mechanical causation throughout nature. In other words, everything happened because of prior causes and conditions (what Aristotle would have called 'efficient causality'). This effectively ruled out Aristotle's 'final cause'; things happened for reasons that lay in the immediate past, not goals that lay in the future.

EXAMPLE

From an Aristotelian perspective, the essence of an acorn is to grow into an oak tree. Its growth is therefore understood in terms of its efforts to actualize that potential.

From a modern scientific perspective, an acorn grows into an oak tree if, and only if, it receives the correct environment to nourish it and it does so on the basis of a genetic code which gives it programmed instructions for how to do it. In a sense, Aristotle is saying 'if you want to understand something, look where it's going', whereas modern science is saying: 'If you want to understand something, look where it has come from and where it is programmed to go.'

In many ways, this freedom from always looking for a final goal and purpose enabled science to make progress, by focusing its attention on antecedent causes and setting out the process of change in a mechanical way, rather than the vaguer language of essences and potentials.

Contrariwise, it started to separate science off from personal and religious views of the world. This did not imply that scientists had no religion. Bacon (along with others, including Newton) tended to speak of the two books written by God, one of revelation and the other of nature. But it had the effect of conveniently distancing religious and personal views from the scientific method.

This meant that science would be free to examine the world in a methodical, rational and impersonal way. But by doing so, it lost the ability to speak directly about what it was examining in a way that was personal and religious. To justify itself, it needed to point, in a utilitarian way, to the benefits it might yield.

A MODERN EXAMPLE

Debates about the right to clone human embryos may include the accusation that science is capable of behaving in ways that do not reflect human values, but only the self-perpetuating process of discovery and experimentation. Those who protest against research may ask 'What is the point? How do we gain by this?' and expect science to justify itself through pointing to an immediate human benefit. Similarly, those who justify research often do so on exactly the same grounds, e.g. that the experimental use of stem cells from cloned embryos may lead to treatments for serious diseases.

Notice now that the distinction between technical questions (what can we find out and what can we do with the information we find?) and personal/religious ones (what is worthwhile? what is the point in this exploration?) can be traced back to this fundamental development of scientific method and the rejection of Aristotle's 'final causes'.

It is interesting, of course, to reflect that the early scientists, very much in the spirit of the Renaissance, believed that all progress in human knowledge was in the long run for the benefit of human life. It was an optimistic period – leading, as they saw it, to a better future, freed from superstition and misery.

Copernicus and Galileo

The change that took place in terms of the use of reason and evidence is well illustrated by the astronomy of the time. **Copernicus** (1473–1543) was a Polish priest, whose views on the nature of the universe were still highly controversial a century after his death. In *De Revolutionibus Orbium*, he claimed that the Sun rather than the Earth was at the centre of the universe and that the Earth rotated every day and revolved around the Sun once a year. He also noted that there was no *stella parallax*, in other words that there was no shift in the relative position of the stars when seen from widely separated places on Earth. He reasoned, from this, that the stars must be considerably further away from the Earth than was the Sun. Clearly, such findings conflicted with the generally accepted cosmology of Ptolemy. When the book was published, it had a preface suggesting that it did not claim to represent the way things actually were in the universe, but merely a convenient alternative way of calculating planetary motion. However, the work did establish that, on the basis of carefully gathered evidence, it was possible to put forward a theory that contradicted the accepted view of the universe.

What Copernicus actually offered was a better explanation of the retrograde motion of the planets, a motion which had to be accounted for by using a complex system of **epicycles** (an epicycle being the path traced by a point on the circumference of one circle as that circle rolls round another one) on the older Ptolemaic system. Nevertheless there were many problems with a Sun-centred model for the universe, if the planets were to move in circular orbits – for at that stage the elliptical orbit was not yet considered – and it is debatable whether Copernicus (who also used the idea of epicycles) actually simplified the calculations that much.

What was more, it could argued that, if the Earth were in fact rotating, we should logically be flung off by its motion and yet there was no evidence on the surface of the Earth that suggested such movement. In replying to these criticisms, his answers were still very Aristotelian. He claimed that evil effects could not follow from a natural movement and that the Earth's motion did not cause a constant wind because the atmosphere, contained 'earthiness' (one of Aristotle's four elements) and therefore revolved in sympathy with the Earth itself. Later, Newton was to explain such things through gravity and the laws of motion, but Copernicus had not made the leap into that new form of scientific thinking.

Hence, it was certainly not the case that Copernicus (and, later, Galileo) stood on one side of a divide with reason and evidence on their side and Aristotelian tradition and religious bigotry on the other. There was a real dilemma about the evidence and its interpretation. In many ways it could have been argued that what Copernicus had produced was that a view of the universe simplified calculations, but did not reflect reality. It was not prejudice that kept Copernicus' theory from acceptance for more than a century, but some real problems that were not resolved. Without a telescope to make his own observations, Copernicus was reliant on naked-eye observations and mathematics.

Note

It would therefore be a fallacy to say that Copernicus instantly revolutionized the way in which people saw the universe or that he enabled reason and observation to triumph. In fact, against much apparent evidence to the contrary, he struggled with the complexity of predicting planetary motion based on the legacy of Ptolemy and wondered if there might be some other way of looking at the evidence.

And herein lies his importance for the philosophy of science, for he recognized that there might be different interpretations of the same evidence, and that it was possible to present two alternative theories and ask which of them was the more useful, which was the simpler and which enabled one to make the best set of predictions.

Copernicus therefore represents a crucial step in a direction which, over the next four centuries, was to transform our way of thinking.

Calculations alone did not yield an easy answer to the structure of the universe. **Brahe** (1546–1601) considered that the planets then known (Mercury, Venus, Mars, Jupiter and Saturn) must move around the Sun, but assumed that the Sun, along with those planets, moved around the Earth. The problem was that such theories were based (and could only be based) on observation of the movements of the planets and Sun relative to Earth, and then sought some explanation to account for them. Galileo (who thought that Brahe's cosmology was wrong, preferring the Copernican system) thought that there was nothing to choose between the systems in terms of such calculations, and hoped to show that the tides would prove that the Earth itself moved and therefore the inherent superiority of the one system over the other.

Kepler (1571–1630) also felt that the tides were significant. He rightly held that they were in some way caused by the Moon, but had no idea of how a body could have an influence at a distance, and was therefore left to speak of the Moon's 'affinity with water'.

His contemporary, Galileo, criticized all such language, declaring that it would have been more honest to say simply that we do not know. Galileo thought the tides must be caused by the movement of the Earth (just as water will slosh around within a bucket when it is moved). His view sounded more rational, but was plainly incorrect.

Kepler, meanwhile, marked yet another radical break with Aristotelian thinking. In observing the orbit of Mars, he found a difference between what he observed and what he calculated should be the case. He concluded that the orbit was elliptical rather than circular, with the Sun at one focus of that ellipse. This contradicted the Aristotelian assumption that perfect motion was circular and therefore heavenly bodies must move in circles. Previous astronomers had tried to retain the perfection of circular motion by suggesting that the orbits of the planets were in fact epicycles.

With **Galileo** (1564–1642), the issues raised by Copernicus were developed in a way that led Einstein to describe him as 'the father of modern physics'. As part of his overall goal to demonstrate that nature operates in a regular, mathematical way, we find him conducting experiments and using instruments to back up his arguments.

A key feature of his work was the use of the telescope, which he developed from the existing spyglass. This showed phenomena that had immediate implications for cosmology. He saw that the 'moving stars' (planets) were not liked the fixed stars, but were orbs, glowing with reflected light. He also observed the phases of Venus, making it quite impossible to accept the cosmology that had been proposed by Ptolemy, since Venus could be seen to go around the Sun. Without observations enhanced by the telescope, there had been no evidence to decide between different interpretations. The only problem at this point was that, although the phases of Venus proved that the Ptolemaic system was wrong, it could not actually prove that the Copernican alternative was correct. True, the evidence was accounted for more simply with that view, but simplicity did not constitute proof.

Of course, as is well known, the Holy Office declared in 1616 that it was a 'revealed truth' (i.e. found in the Bible) that the Sun moved round the Earth, but Galileo got round this by agreeing with his then friend Pope Urban VIII to consider Copernicus only as a useful hypothesis, of value for astrological calculations. This was in fact not an unreasonable attitude to take, mainly because neither Galileo nor anyone else could see any possibility of gaining absolute proof one way or the other.

In 1632, Galileo published his *Dialogue of the Two Chief World Systems* in which he directly compared Copernicus' view with that of Ptolemy and came to the conclusion that Copernicus was right. The implication of this work was that Copernicus had described the actual universe and not simply offered a useful hypothesis for making calculations – thus going directly against Galileo's earlier agreement with the Pope.

The matter was made rather more complex because Galileo used the dialogue form, in which two characters present the alternative world systems and a third tries to judge between them. This enabled him to present the case for Copernicus through the mouth of his character Salviati, without actually saying that he endorsed it himself. He was, in using the dialogue form, expressing the fundamental problem of his day, that of the varied approaches to evidence and authority.

Against the charge that, if the Earth moved, one would feel the movement, Galileo argued that no experiment conducted on the Earth could ever prove its movement. He cites the example of a large ship. If one is in an inner cabin of a large ship, there is no sense of motion. Equally, butterflies or fish in such a cabin could move normally, quite oblivious of the larger movement of the ship, in which they were being carried. Hence, on the surface of the Earth, there would be no evidence for its motion.

Of course, in the end it is clear that the dialogue is not evenly balanced; the Copernican side prevails. The movement of the planets, the annual shifting of the path of sunspots and the tides all suggest that the Earth in fact (not just in theory) moves around the Sun rather than the other way around. And this, of course, then brought Galileo into conflict with the officially agreed position.

Galileo was put on trial and forced to recant. He had used reason and observation to challenge the literal interpretation of scripture and the authority of the Church. Although it is popular to see this as a significant moment when authority was challenged by scientific evidence and reacted with authoritative high-handedness, it was far from straightforward. Much was still unproved, and religious and scientific communities were both divided on the issues. Neither did it mean that he received no support from the Church. It is clear that a significant number of senior Churchmen (including the Pope Urban VIII) had earlier been supportive of his work. One prelate had written an apology to Galileo after a priest had criticized him from the pulpit for propounding views that contradicted the literal meaning of scripture. The prelate was clearly irritated by the naive and literalist approach taken by the priest.

Two important goals for Galileo were rational explanation and simplicity. So, for example, in his work on motion, particularly looking at the path followed by projectiles, Galileo worked out theoretically why a 45° angle enabled a gunner to achieve the greatest range. This was known from practical experience, of course, and could be reproduced by experiment; but such experimental method was only a means to the end of a rational explanation of how something worked. This, of course, was to become the distinguishing feature of the whole of what we tend to refer to as Newtonian science, the framing of laws by which the actual motions and behaviour of objects can be understood and predicted.

His other aim was simplicity. Consider the view of the universe taken by Ptolemy on the one hand and Pythagoras/Copernicus on the other. On the Ptolemaic system, not only the Sun, but the planets and all the fixed stars were required to move around the Earth once every day. How much simpler it would be if the same appearance of motion were possible with only the Earth moving. Equally, the movement of sunspots – which were observed carefully by Galileo – required the Sun to go through a complex set of gyrations in order to explain why the path of the spots was either convex or concave when viewed from the Earth on all but two days in the year. Much easier to assume that it was the Earth's movement that meant that the path of the spots was being observed from a tilting Earth.

If there are particular moments in the history of science in which there are major philosophical breakthroughs, the later work of Galileo is one of them. In presenting his book on *Two New Sciences* (being the sciences of materials and of motion) which was published in 1638, he made this astounding statement:

> The cause of the acceleration of the motion of falling bodies is not a necessary part of the investigation.

Now this has important implications. According to Aristotle, one should seek the cause of a particular phenomenon – asking why it has happened and what its significance was (as we have seen in his idea of the four causes). What Galileo was saying was that he was examining the actual way in which something happened, not why it happened. Ultimate explanations were thus removed from the realm of science.

Galileo backed up his work by setting up experimental demonstrations. Earlier in his career he had dropped balls of different weights from the top of the Leaning Tower of Pisa in order to demonstrate that things accelerate downwards at the same speed. In actual fact, it didn't work quite as he had planned, since added wind resistance meant that the different balls struck the ground at slightly different times – but in any case they were much closer than would have been predicted by Aristotle, who thought that bodies accelerated towards the Earth in proportion to their weight.

The Newtonian world-view

In his key work, *Philosophiae Naturalis Principia Mathematica*, **Sir Isaac Newton** (1642–1727) examines the world along mathematical principles. With absolute time and space and laws of motion which determined the movement of all bodies, refining concepts such as mass, force, velocity and acceleration, he provided a comprehensive framework for the development of physics. His was the definining voice of science until challenged in the 20th century. Even now, whereas it is recognized that his physics is inadequate for examining the extremes of scale in the universe, whether cosmic or sub-atomic, it is the basic laws of motion set down by Newton that are the practical guide for the majority of ordinary physical calculations and which have given rise to the majority of technologies that shape our lives.

Where Aristotle would have said that an object seeks its natural place within the universe, Newton's First Law states that it remains in a state of rest or in uniform motion in a straight line unless acted upon by a force. No overall theory of purpose or end, therefore, but one of forces bringing about change. The universe for Newton is pushed, not pulled; it is the past and not the future that determines what will happen.

The massive contribution of Newton does not rest only on the laws of motion, however radical they proved to be, but in the general view of the universe as a rational and understandable place, whose every operation could be plotted and expressed in mathematical terms. The world of Newton was perhaps (from the standpoint of the 21st century) small, crude and mechanical; but it represented a basis upon which – for the next 200 years – there could be serious developments in both theoretical science and practical technology.

With the coming of the Newtonian world, philosophy changed its function, from permitting metaphysical speculations about the nature of reality, to examining the logic of the newly formulated principles and justifying their acceptance in terms of looking at scientific method. In particular, it was with the work of Immanuel Kant that it became recognized that these Newtonian laws were not simply 'out there' in the world, but were fundamentally a feature of the way in which the human mind encounters and makes sense of its experience.

Comment

In this section, we have outlined the popular view that the rise of modern science ousted the work of Aristotle and that the scientists of the 16th to 18th centuries were battling with the authority given to his philosophy, supported forcefully by the Catholic Church.

This is true only to a certain extent. In actual fact, Aristotle (and other ancient philosophers) continued to be studied and were an important influence long after those developments that we refer to as the 'rise of modern science'. The key feature, however (as we see in the work of Bacon and Descartes, for example) is that Aristotle's 'four causes', were effectively reduced to two: 'material' and 'efficient'. The effect of this was to portray the world as a machine, essentially comprised of physical objects causally related to one another. What is lost is Aristotle's 'formal cause' – that which gives shape and coherence to a complex entity – and his 'final cause' which is its overall purpose and aim.

In other words, in the movement from Ancient Greek and mediaeval thought to the modern period, we see a reduction in the ways in which it was deemed appropriate to consider an object and its nature with respect to the rest of the world. It is essentially now a mechanism – matter in motion. The concentration on 'efficient causation', unhindered by other considerations, enabled great advances to take place in terms of the prediction of physical events and the framing of scientific laws. Those parts of Aristotle that it no longer took into account became 'metaphysics', seen as the realm of philosophy of religion.

We should not forget the enormous significance of other figures in the history of science. Boyle, for example, who at the end of the 17th century did fundamental work in chemistry, showing how elements combine to form compounds; or, more than a century later, the work of Dalton in examining the way atoms combine to form molecules.

There was a steady development of scientific theories and also in the establishment of science: both The Royal Society in England and the Académie des Sciences in France were founded in the 17th century.

New instruments promoted the careful examination of the world: the telescope, invented in the early years of the 17th century and developed by Galileo and used by him to controversial effect. Microscopes were also being developed and by the latter part of the century, Robert Hooke's *Micrographia* was fascinating people by showing images of things previously far too small to be observed. The 17th century saw the development of the pendulum clock by Christian Huygens and, by the mid-18th century, John Harrison was perfecting his timepiece to achieve an accurate calculation of longitude, an invaluable aid for those travelling by sea. Twenty years later the Montgolfier brothers had taken their first manned balloon flight (1783) and by the end of the century Count Volta had produced the electric battery.

Perception and reality

The Newtonian world-view was underpinned by fundamental changes in the way philosophers perceived the world. **Thomas Hobbes** (1588–1679) took a materialist view of reality, arguing that a concept such as 'incorporeal substance' was self-contradictory. Everything that exists must have some physical form. Even the mind was seen as a machine and thoughts were but movement of matter inside the brain. In short, everything is matter in a state of motion.

There were also debates about the nature and reliability of human perception. Locke was to distinguish between **primary** and **secondary qualities** – an important distinction for science. Others (e.g. Descartes) questioned the reality of experience in the quest for certainty.

While not part of the philosophy of science itself – which, at the time of these thinkers, had not emerged as a separate area of study – philosophical discussions of the nature of reality and of perception are an important backdrop to the developing sciences.

19th-century developments

The changes brought about by science and technology in the 19th century were quite amazing. The early decades saw the dominance of steam power – in railways, factories, steam ships and pumps. But from the 1830s another form of power was to transform technology: electricity. First the dynamo and motor, then the electric telegraph, offering instant international communications, with a transatlantic cable operative from 1866.

Then, with Bell's invention of the telephone in 1876, and Marconi's radio transmission in 1895, the world was set for a revolution in personal communication.

With the telephone, telegraph, a postal service, steam railways, factories, buildings constructed using steel and the arrival of the motor car in 1885, the world had been transformed. By the end of the century, life and health could be improved by taking Aspirin and having an X-ray, or could be ended by a machine gun or an electric chair. Although there was a moral and romantic reaction against the 'dark satanic mills' of the Industrial Revolution, it is difficult to imagine that towards the end of the 19th century many could seriously have challenged the overall benefits to humankind offered by science and technology – it had become fundamental to the whole way of life in developed countries. And, of course, in terms of the perceptions of life in general, it seemed to offer humankind the prospect of increasing mastery over its environment.

The sciences of humankind

As we shall see in a moment, the biggest single change in human self-understanding to come from the 19th century was brought about by the theory of evolution. But alongside this was another, less obvious, but equally important development: the use of statistics. Today we take it for granted that any examination of personal or social life will be set against a background of statistical information. For example, in order to study possible environmental factors in the incidence of disease, we look at statistics for the disease in various environments or among people who do certain work or have a particular habit (like smoking, taking no exercise). On the basis of these, evidence is put forward in the form of 'people who do X are 80% more likely to contract Y'. Thus we often accept statistical correlations as good evidence for one thing causing another, even where the actual way in which it causes it is unknown.

The modern sciences of humankind – psychology, sociology, political science, social science – are quite unthinkable without a foundation of information gathered in the form of statistics. But it was only in the 19th century that humankind started to became the object of study in this way.

As these statistics were analysed, for example, by the sociologist **Durkheim** (1858–1917), it became evident that there were trends in human behaviour that could be measured and predicted. Durkheim came to the conclusion that there were social 'laws' at work that could be known statistically, since they produced sufficient pressure on individuals to account for a certain number of them following a particular line of action. Of course, it was not assumed (either then or now) that statistics could show laws of the same sort as the laws of physics. There was no way that individual choice could be determined by them. But it was argued that, at the social level and in sufficiently large numbers, behaviour could be mapped and predicted.

As we shall see later, this had implications for an understanding of freedom. If there are statistical laws, are those who go to make up the statistics, on which they are based, really free? Are they forced (at least to some extent) to follow a social trend, even if they are unaware of it?

On the political side, this period also saw the work of **Karl Marx** (1818–1883), who, through analyses of historical causes of conflict and relating them to the class structure of society, was able to look at the political and social arena in terms of political laws. Thus he appeared to offer a 'science' of humankind's behaviour in this sphere. As will be seen later, some 20th-century philosophers (e.g. Popper) were to criticize Marxism as pseudo-science on the grounds that it did not allow contradictory evidence to determine whether its theories were right or wrong, but simply adapted its interpretation to take all possibilities into account. Nevertheless, with Marx we do have a theory which purports to use scientific method to study mankind – and, of course, not just to understand the way things are, but to change them.

Thus we find that the attention of science has been turned towards humankind, and that human behaviour becomes open to study and scientific analysis. As we have already noted, the key problem with this was the issue of human freedom. If I sense that I am a free individual, how can a social scientist tell me that my response to life is predictable?

But there remained an enormous issue in terms of 19th-century science and self-understanding, one that appeared to get at the very core of what is meant to be a human being, supreme over lesser species – and that was the theory of evolution.

The challenge of evolution

The work on evolution, leading up to that of **Charles Darwin** (1809–1882), took two forms: an examination of interpretation of fossil evidence and theories about how species might develop.

William Smith (1769–1839) studied rock strata and the fossils contained in them. He recognized that the deeper and older strata showed life forms different from those found in the present and concluded that there must have been many successive acts of creation. Geology had emerged as a science capable of revealing history.

The same evidence led **Charles Lyall**, in his book *Principles of Geology* (published between 1830 and 1833) to a different view. He argued for a continuous process of change, rather than separate acts of creation, to account for the differences between the layers of fossils. His view was termed 'uniformitarianism'. What he did not have, of course, was an understanding of the mechanism that could drive such change – but neither did Chambers in his controversial book *The Vestiges of the Natural History of Creation*, published anonymously in 1844. Its view that new species could appear, challenged both the biblical account of creation but also the sense that humankind might have a unique place within the scheme of things.

Other scientists were already framing the ideas that led more directly to Darwin's understanding of evolution. His grandfather, **Erasmus Darwin** (1731–1802), thought that all organic life formed a single living filament over the Earth and that new species could develop from old. He saw humankind as the culmination of evolution, but not separate from it. His book *Zoonomia* (1794) was mainly a medical textbook, but it included his ideas about evolution. In many ways, his thinking anticipated that of his grandson.

A key figure in the rise of evolutionary theory was **Jean Baptiste de Lamark** (1744–1829). He believed that you could categorize species in terms of their complexity, with every species tending to evolve into something more complex. The way in which this happened, according to Lamark, was through offspring inheriting the characteristics which an individual had developed during his or her lifetime. In other words, a person who had developed a particular strength or ability would be able to conceive a child who had that same quality and thus move evolution in that direction. This (generally known as the 'Theory of Acquired Characteristics') became a widely held view during the 19th century, to be overtaken by Charles Darwin's alternative explanation in terms of natural selection.

Another scientist who had a profound impact on the emerging idea of evolution was **Thomas Malthus** (1766–1834). He observed that, in any situation where there were limited supplies of food, the populations of species would be limited. Within the species, there would be competition to get such food as was available, as a result of which only those who were strongest, or in some other way best able to get at the food, would survive. These observations, set out in his *Essays on the Principle of Population* (1798) were to provide Charles Darwin with the mechanism he needed to explain the process of evolution.

The breakthrough in the scientific understanding of evolution came with Charles Darwin himself. His *Origin of Species* (1859) was controversial because it presented for the first time a theory (natural selection) by which one species could develop from another. His story is well known. He was convinced, by the variety of the species he had seen, especially on the Galapagos Islands in the early 1830s, by the way they were adapted to their surroundings, and by the way in which some living species were related to fossils, that one species must indeed develop out of another. He worked for the next 20 years to develop the theory of how this took place.

Darwin was well aware of the ability of farmers and others to breed particular forms of animals. It was clear that, by selecting particular individuals for breeding, a species could be gradually changed.

He noticed, when on the Galapagos Islands, the way in which finches on different islands tended to have different beaks in relation to the type of food available. He concluded that there had been just a single form of finch originally, but that on each of the islands the isolated communities of finches had each developed in response to those characteristics which gave them an advantage in terms of gathering food. If you needed a short stubby beak for cracking nuts, then that was the characteristic that tended to dominate in the breeding stakes.

This, of course, served to reinforce what Malthus had said about the control of population numbers through finite food supplies. Variation and the overall limitation of food thus gave Darwin what he needed for his theory about the mechanism of evolutionary change. In his theory of 'natural selection', Darwin argued:

- Some individuals within a species have characteristics that help them to survive better than others.
- Those who survive to adulthood are likely to breed and thus pass on their characteristics to the next generation.
- Thus, with successive generations, there will be an increase within a species of those characteristics which improve its chances of survival.
- The characteristics of a species are thus gradually modified to facilitate survival.

In effect, Darwin had suggested that the environment within which any species lived had carried out, in a natural and mechanical way, what farmers and breeders had long been doing to domestic animals – it had selected favoured characteristics for breeding.

The first four chapters of *Origin of Species* outline the process by which his theory is established. He starts with looking at the process of breeding domesticated animals. Then he moves on to consider the variety within species in the wild. He links this with Malthus, by exploring the struggle for existence. Then, from this, he is able to formulate the theory of 'natural selection'.

With hindsight, given what had been examined before Darwin, the theory seems obvious, a gathering together of insights that had already been explored by others. In fact, however, it was the clarity of the argument in *Origin of Species* that made it so crucial in shifting the whole way of thinking about evolution. What he had produced was a convincing argument about the mechanism by which evolution could take place, a mechanism which was impersonal and certainly required no divine designer to bring it about. It also placed humankind on a level with all the other species, for it too had emerged through a process of natural selection.

Comment

Of course, our knowledge of genetics has now shown the random process of errors which occur when genes are copied, some of which may be beneficial. Evolution is a theory which is at once, elegant, simple, but devastatingly mechanical. In it, Aristotle's 'final causation' can have no place – what appears as design or purpose, is but the operation of cumulative chance. Hardly surprising that Darwin theory proved so controversial.

Later Darwin was to go on to explore the implications of this for humankind. His books dealing specifically with human evolution are *The Descent of Man* (1871) and *Expressions of the Emotions in Man and Animals* (1872). But, from the perspective of the history of science, it is *Origin of Species* that marks the decisive step.

Relativity and thermodynamics

Having overthrown the overarching authority of Aristotle in the mediaeval world-view, science, by the latter part of the 19th century seemed to have become established on absolutely solid foundations, based clearly on reason and evidence. Some (e.g. the philosopher Haeckel, who in *The Riddle of the Universe* (1899) proposed a philosophy of scientific materialism) believed that little still remained to be discovered; Newtonian physics and Darwinian evolution had, between them, provided a secure framework for answering scientific questions, which – by implication – were the only ones worth asking.

All that was, of course, swept away by the discoveries of the early 20th century. Once again, authority was challenged – but this time it was the authority of Newtonian physics that came under attack. The philosophy of science suddenly had to open up to the possibility that there may be equally valid but contradictory ways of understanding phenomena. The general perception of science also changed, from what might have been seen as the triumph of common-sense reason and evidence in the 17th century, to the acceptance of ideas that seemed far removed from logic and common sense. The world, in the 20th century, was revealed as a far more confusing and complex place that had been thought a century earlier.

Note

It would be quite impossible to summarize here all the major developments in science that have taken place during the 20th century, neither is it necessary for the purposes of understanding the philosophy of science. What we need to grasp are the key features that distinguish recent developments from the earlier world of Newtonian physics and the implications they have for understanding the way science goes about its task and justifies its results.

Relativity

The two theories of relativity, developed by **Albert Einstein** (1879–1955) in the early years of the 20th century, showed the limitations of Newtonian physics. 'Special relativity', which he put forward in 1905, may be summarized in the equation $E=mc^2$. It links mass and energy. *E* stands for energy, *m* for mass and *c* for the speed of light. The equation shows that a small mass is equivalent to a large amount of energy.

'General relativity', which followed in 1916, argued that space, time, mass and energy were all linked. A famous prediction made by this theory was that, a strong gravitational field would bend rays of light and this was confirmed soon afterwards by observing the apparent shift of location of stars during an eclipse of the sun (see page 45). Both space and time are influenced by gravity. Space is compressed and time speeds up as gravity increases. But gravity is proportional to mass (the larger the mass, the greater its gravitational pull) and, according to the theory of special relativity, mass is related to energy.

The implications of all this is to deny a single or definitive perspective. In observing something, the position and movement of the observer has to be taken into account. It might have been adequate in Newton's day to assume a static position on Earth from which things could be observed, but Einstein effectively showed that there was no one fixed point; everything is relative.

It also had the effect of setting the limit to any known process or connection: the speed of light. If two objects are moving apart at a speed greater than the speed of light, they can have no connection with one another. The speed of light therefore determines the dimensions of the known universe.

Newtonian physics was still considered valid, but only within a narrow set of parameters.

Thermodynamics

The fundamental interconnectedness of all physical states, shown by relativity, is illustrated also by the three laws of thermodynamics.

The First Law of Thermodynamics states that there is a conservation of mass-energy; the one may be turned into the other, but the sum total of the two remains constant. The Second Law is that in every process there is some loss of energy and heat. Therefore, as organized or complex things interact, they gradually give off energy and therefore tend to become cooler and less organized. In other words, everything (and that means the whole universe) is gradually moving in a direction of general disorder or entropy.

> **Note**
>
> In looking at this general drift towards entropy, there is a difference between open and closed systems. In a closed system, everything gradually winds down as energy is dissipated. An open system (i.e. one which has the capacity to take into itself energy from outside) can be self-sustaining and can grow to become more complex. Thus individual parts of the world can be seen to 'warm up', while the universe as a whole – which by definition must be a closed system – is 'cooling down'.

The Third Law of Thermodynamics shows that the cooler something is the less energy it can produce and that all energy ceases to be produced at a temperature of –273° Kelvin. This again sets a limit to the universe: at absolute zero, everything stops.

In Newtonian physics, because it was concerned with a limited set of conditions as found on Earth, these fundamental limits did not apply. Thermodynamics shows that the universe is not a piece of machinery in perpetual motion; every process is paid for by the dissipation of energy.

The impact of quantum mechanics

The debate about quantum mechanics, particularly that between Einstein and Bohr conducted in the 1930s, raised fundamental issues about what science can say and is therefore of great interest to the philosophy of science.

Quantum mechanics developed in an examination of sub-atomic phenomena and therefore concerned issues that could not arise before the early 20th century. The idea that matter was composed of atoms separated from one another by empty space was not new, having been put forward by Leucippus and Democritus in the 5th century BCE (see page 3). But until the discovery of the electron in 1897, the atom had been thought of as a solid but indivisible speck of physical matter. The atom was then visualized as having a nucleus made up of protons and neutrons, with electrons circling round it, like planets in a solar system. Once it reached that stage, theories were developed about sub-atomic particles, their behaviour and relationship to one another. Matter was soon to be seen as particles bound together by nuclear forces.

Note

The term 'quantum mechanics' came from the work of Max Planck, who found that radiation (e.g. light or energy) came in small measurable increments or packets ('quanta') rather than as a continuous stream.

When dealing with things that cannot be observed directly, it is difficult to decide if an image, or way of describing it, is adequate or not. You cannot simply point to the actual thing and make a comparison! Hence, when dealing with sub-atomic particles, all imagery is going to be limited.

A major problem was that particles seemed to change, depending upon how they were observed. Unlike the predictable world of Newtonian physics, quantum theory claimed that you could not predict the action of individual particles. At most, you could describe them in terms of probabilities. Observing large numbers, you could say what percentage were likely to do one thing rather than another, but it was impossible to say that of any one particular particle.

In 1927, **Heisenberg** showed that the more accurately the position of a particle is measured, the more difficult it is to predict its velocity (and vice versa). You can know one or the other, but not both at the same time. But was this 'uncertainty principle' a feature of reality itself or did it simply reflect the limitation of our ability to observe and measure what was happening at this sub-atomic level?

As we shall see later (page 83) this led to considerable debate about the way in which quantum theory should be interpreted. In particular, the issue that divided Einstein and **Niels Bohr** (1885–1962) was whether quantum theory showed what was actually the case, or simply what we could or could not observe to be the case. (Bohr held the former position, but Einstein refused to accept that actual events could be random.) An example of this issue is presented in the well-known thought-experiment called 'Schrodinger's Cat' (see page 84).

In other words

The issue here is quite fundamental. In traditional mechanics and statistics, we may not be able to know the action of individual things (any more than we can know what an individual voter is going to do at an election), although we can predict general trends. But at the same time, it is believed that each individual is actually determined, although we cannot know all the factors involved or cannot measure them. Quantum mechanics goes against this, saying that everything is a matter of probability and that it is never going to be possible, even in theory, to know the actual behaviour of individual particles.

Genetics

It is difficult to gauge the full extent of the revolution that has sprung from the discovery of the structure of DNA, made by Francis Crick and James Watson in 1953. It has provided a remarkable way of exploring, relating and (controversially) manipulating living forms. In many ways the genetic basis for life is the archetypal scientific discovery; the structure that carries the instructions from which all living things are formed. It has revolutionized the biological sciences in the same way that relativity and quantum mechanics have revolutionized physics.

Briefly, deoxyribonucleic acid (DNA) is made up of two strands of chemical units called nucleotides, spiralled into a double helix. These chemical units come in sequences (the genes) which give the instructions for how the amino acids in proteins are to put together living cells. Human DNA is found in 23 pairs of chromosomes in the nucleus of a cell. Thus the 'genetic' information, contained in the DNA, determines the character of every organism.

This has many implications for the philosophy of biology, and the potential uses of genetics raise questions of a more general metaphysical and ethical nature. As we saw earlier, Darwin's theory of natural selection depended on the idea that there would always be small variations between individuals of a species and that those with particular advantages would survive to breed. What Darwin did not know was the mechanism for these random variations. We now know that it is because the genetic code is not always copied exactly, leading to mutations, some of which survive and reproduce. Such mistakes are rare, and they can only be passed onto offspring when they occur in particular cells. Nevertheless, genetics has endorsed Darwin's theory, by showing how variations can occur and thereby giving the raw material upon which his 'natural selection' can go to work.

Another important consequence of genetics is the recognition of the similarity between all living things. We find that similar genes perform similar tasks in very different species, showing that they have a common ancestry.

SUMMARY

The overall effect of the genetic revolution in biology is to turn evolution from a theory that lacked adequate fossil evidence into a fact that cannot be ignored. All living things share the same genetic basis. This in itself brings about a radical interconnectedness of things. We shall examine some of the implications of modern work on genetics, particularly the human genome, in Chapters 7 and 8.

Some implications

An understanding of genetics is relevant not merely to examining the way in which science operates and the philosophy related to the appearance of design and purpose in nature (an area where it touches on the philosophy of religion) but also in matters of ethics. It is one thing to say that something can be done, quite another to argue that is should be done.

EXAMPLE

In January 2001, the UK government approved the use of cloned embryos for medical research. It was argued that they were needed for stem cell research, which might lead to the development of replacement cells for many degenerative diseases. Other people protested about any use of cloned embryos, arguing that such cloning of human cells might lead eventually to the cloning of human beings and particularly to the production of 'designer babies', matched to parental wishes in terms of genetic make-up, which might include all elements, including intelligence and appearance.

The issue here is the extent to which pure science should be limited by the implications of technologies to which it may give rise. This has always been a problem and no doubt there are some environmentalists who deeply regret the development of the internal combustion engine! Certainly there are those (including Einstein himself) who were desperately concerned about the development of their research in the production of nuclear weapons. By way of contrast, thinkers such as Archimedes, made a point of using his knowledge specifically to develop weaponry.

A fundamental issue here is that science operates at an impersonal level, correctly pointing out that life is basically organized according to genetic information. This may be so, but it does not correspond to the experienced world, where an individual is felt to be somehow special, not simply a product of this certain genetic code. The fear is that the use of science here will create problems that belong to the personal and moral realm, rather than that of science itself.

Comment

One is unlikely now to want to reject all the benefits of modern medicine, communication or travel. At what point, then, are we able to say that an area of research is unlikely to lead to an improvement in the quality of human life? And should that be the ultimate factor in determining the viability of a research programme? At this point, the normal issues with which the philosophy of science is concerned give way to ethics and politics. However, it would seem curious to study the one, without being aware of the implications of the subject for those other areas of human concern.

The digital revolution

Computing is not new, but previously it was time consuming: there is a physical limit to what can be done with an abacus! The first steps towards modern computing were taken by **Charles Babbage** in 1820, who hit upon the idea of devising a mechanical device for mathematical computation. Although his initial efforts were not well received, he persisted, using ideas for inputting data by punch card and other features that were to become part of modern computing.

A real breakthrough in computing came with the work of **Alan Turing** (1912–1954). The crucial practical difference between his work and the earlier efforts of Babbage was the use of simple digital technology and the recognition that all that was required was a binary (off/on) device, such as a telephone relay. When a complex mathematical question was broken down into a sequence of binary choices, a machine could perform each of those operations and therefore by the application of logic, could solve problems. The work received a great boost through the efforts to break Nazi codes during World War II. Turing's 'universal machine' contributed to the code breaking at Bletchley Park, which gave the allies invaluable information about enemy intentions.

By the first year of the 21st century, children were playing on computers far more powerful than anything used in the NASA space programme that put a man on the moon 30 years earlier. But alongside that has come the crucial ability to network computers and through that, what may turn out to be the most significant of all technological developments – the Internet. In spite of all the problems of control and the issues related to the provision and distribution of material that may be deemed harmful, there can be no doubt that life is perceived quite differently by those who routinely use it as a source of instant information from any part of the globe and the ability to communicate, contribute and relate to people and institutions anywhere. It is very difficult to get the Internet into perspective, simply because it is so new and is changing so fast, but there can be no doubt about its social impact.

The development of computing is perhaps the most immediately obvious aspect of the digital revolution, but the issue, certainly as far as the philosophy of science is concerned, goes much deeper. Whereas in the 17th and 18th centuries mathematics was an important feature in the developing sciences, it was used primarily as a tool of logic. And that has continued to be the case. From cosmology to nuclear physics, mathematics is a fundamental tool of scientific work. Then, as we saw, from the 19th century, statistics started to be gathered and analysed. This gave social scientists and others a way of making causal connections that had the backing of large numbers of observations, expressed in terms of probabilities. Statistics became a tool of analysis.

Then, with the ability to manipulate vast quantities of information in digital form, it became possible to use digital technology not just as an aid to calculation but also to use it as a way of analysing and expressing fundamental features of reality.

The digital revolution has changed almost all aspects of life. In photography, for example, the detail that could previously only be recorded on a light-sensitive photographic emulsion can now we recorded digitally. The resulting picture 'is' a sequence of binary bits. Sound can equally be analysed, stored and transmitted more accurately in digital form than through earlier mechanical or analogue form. And, of course, with the human genome, the most fundamental aspects of life itself are expressible in digital code.

A DVD disk can store sound, film, a multi-volume encyclopaedia or the genetic instructions for creating living tissue. And all these things, which are (in human terms) *experienced* very differently, are *expressed* in exactly the same way – by a sequence of binary code, a sequence of off/on gate switches.

The fundamental implication of this would be quite astounding, were it not so commonplace now, thanks to technology. Reality is built up through a sequence of pieces of information. Everything may be reduced to, and then reconstructed from, the most basic of all forms, a sequence of binary code.

Postscript

This brief survey of some aspects of the history of science started with the pre-Socratics and their speculation about the fundamental constituents of reality. Thales observed the world carefully and came to the view that water was the fundamental component in everything; today we are conducting the same process, using analytic methods not available to Thales and coming to the conclusion that everything can be expressed in the form of digital information.

2 THE SCIENTIFIC METHOD

In this chapter, we shall look at the basic approach to science that developed from the 17th century and which may still be used to some extent to distinguish between genuine science and pseudoscience. We will be concerned mainly with the inductive method of gaining knowledge and the impact it had on scientific methodology. The key feature here is the recognition that all claims to scientific knowledge must be supported by evidence from observation and/or experiment.

Subsequent chapters will then develop this in terms of 20th-century debates about how scientific theories are developed, assessed and replaced and the more general problem of scientific realism – in other words, whether scientific statements do in fact describe what is the case 'out there' in the objective, physical world, rather than what is going on within our perceiving minds. A key question in all this is whether scientific theories can ever be proved to be correct, in any absolute sense, by the evidence that supports them.

In other words, the rise of modern science brought with it an ideal about what constituted certain knowledge; modern debates show that, although it may remain an ideal, it is very difficult (perhaps impossible) to achieve fully in practice.

Observation and objectivity

Caution is a keynote in making scientific claims. Everything that is said should be backed up by sound theoretical reasoning and experimental evidence. Here, for example, is a statement made by Professor Neil Turok in 1998, in a newspaper article describing his work with Professor Stephen Hawking on the early states of the universe, It contains two very wise notes of caution:

First, the discovery is essentially mathematical, and is formulated in the language of the theory of general relativity invented by Albert Einstein to describe gravity, the force which shapes the large scale structure of the universe. It is hard to describe such things in everyday terms without being misleading in some respects – the origin of our universe was certainly not an everyday event.

The second important warning I have to give is that the theories we have built of a very early universe before the Big Bang are not yet backed up by experiment. We often talk as if they are real because we take them very seriously, but we certainly have no special oracular insight to the truth. What we are doing is constructing hypotheses which conform to the very rigorous standard of theoretical physics. But we are under no illusions that, until our theories are thoroughly supported by detailed experimental and observatory results they will remain speculative.

(*Daily Telegraph*, March 14 1998)

Notice two important points here:

- It is not always possible to describe things in language which will enable a non-scientist to get an accurate, imaginative grasp of what is being discussed. Some things are so extraordinary that they make sense only in terms of mathematical formulas. There are occasions when scientists have claimed that they were able to visualize something before expressing it in scientific terms, but often that is not the case.
- Second – and this will be central to our discussion of scientific method in this chapter – every claim needs to be backed up by evidence. Such evidence may take the form of observations of a natural phenomenon, especially in the case of astronomy, or natural selection, where populations of a particular species need to be measured and their characteristics noted. But more often the evidence to support theories comes from the results of experiments that are set up to measure a particular aspect of reality that the scientist wants to explore.

Experiments

In much of this chapter we shall be concerned with evidence and how it is assessed. However, we need to keep in mind that, in science, much of what it presented as evidence is not observation, but the results of experiment. Experiments create an artificial situation which eliminates the factors that appear to be of no consequence to the thing that is being examined, so that the investigator can focus on and measure a single, or small number of variables. The resulting information is more precise and controlled and may therefore be useful in formulating a theory, but it does not reflect what happens in the 'real' world, where everything is interconnected and mixed, with a theoretically infinite number of influences operating upon it.

No experiment can ever show the whole situation; if it did, it would have to be as large and complex as the universe. Experimental evidence is therefore highly selective and may reflect the assumptions of the scientist. This, as we shall see later in this book, is the root cause of much of the debate about the status of scientific theories.

One debate concerns whether there can be crucial experiments, which are decisive in saying which of a number of competing theories is correct. Early scientists (e.g. Francis Bacon) thought this possible, but others (e.g. Pierre Duhem, a physicist writing at the end of the 19th century and the first years of the 20th) have argued that they are impossible, since you can never know the sum total of possible theories that can be applied to any set of experimental results. For practical purposes however, some experiments (e.g. the observations that confirmed Einstein's general relativity – see page 45) do appear to be decisive in saying that, of existing theories, one is superior to the others.

As we saw in the historical survey, when Galileo argued in favour of the Copernican view of the universe, in which the Earth revolved around the Sun rather than vice versa, his work was challenged by the more conservative thinkers of his day, not because his observations or calculations were found to be at wrong, but because his argument was based on those observations and calculations, rather than on a theoretical understanding of the principles that should govern a perfectly ordered universe.

Galileo struggled against a background of religious authority which gave Aristotelian ideas of perfection and purpose priority over observations and experimental evidence. He performed experiments to show that Aristotelian theory was wrong. In other words, the earlier medieval system of thought was deductive – it deduced what should happen from its ideas, in contrast to Galileo's inductive method of getting to a theory from observations, experiments and calculations. This inductive method is a key feature in the establishment of the scientific method of gaining knowledge.

The other key difference between the experiments and observations carried out by Galileo and the older Aristotelian view of reality was that Galileo simply looked at what happened, not at why it happened.

We have already seen (on page 11) that this was a key feature of the work of Francis Bacon, who rejected Aristotle's idea of final causes and insisted that knowledge should be based on evidence. His 'idols' of habit, prejudice and conformity and his insistence that one should accept evidence even where it did not conform to one's expectations mark a clear shift to what became established as the scientific method.

Experience and knowledge

A crucial step in appreciating scientific method comes with recognizing, and attempting to eliminate, those elements in what we see that come from our ways of seeing, rather from the external reality that we are looking at.

The philosopher **John Locke** (1632–1704) argued that everything we know derives from sense experience. When we perceive an object, we describe it as having certain qualities. Locke divided these qualities into two categories:

- Primary qualities belonged to the object itself and included its location, its dimensions and its mass. He considered that these would remain true for the object no matter who perceived it.

- Secondary qualities depended upon the sense faculties of the person perceiving the object and could vary with circumstances. Thus, for example, the ability to perceive colour, smell and sound depends upon our senses; if the light changes, we see things as having a different colour.

Science was therefore concerned with primary qualities. These it could measure, and seemed to be objective, as opposed to the more subjective secondary ones.

Comment

Imagine how different the world would be if examined only in terms of primary qualities. Rather than colours, sounds and tastes, you would have information about dimensions. Music would be a digital sequence or the pulsing of sound waves in the air. A sunset would be information about wavelengths of light and the composition of the atmosphere.

In general, science deals with primary qualities. The personal encounter with the world, taking in a multitude of experiences simultaneously, mixing personal interpretation and the limitations of sense experience with whatever is encountered as external to the self, is the stuff of the arts, not of science.

Science analyses, eliminates the irrelevant and the personal and finds the relationship between the primary qualities of objects.

Setting aside the dominance of secondary qualities in experience, along with any sense of purpose or goal, was essential for the development of scientific method – but it was not an easy step to take. The mechanical world of Newtonian physics was a rather abstract and dull place – far removed from the confusing richness of personal experience.

As we shall see again later, one thing that becomes clear the more we look at the way in which information is gathered and the words and images used to describe it, is that there will always be a gap between reality and description. Just as the world changes depending on whether we are mainly concerned with primary or secondary qualities, so the pictures and models we use to describe it cannot really be said to be 'true', simply because there is no way to make a direct comparison between the model and the reality to which it points. Our experience cannot be unambiguous, because it depends on so many personal factors. Scientific method developed in order to eliminate those personal factors and therefore to achieve knowledge based simply on reason and evidence.

Note

Even instruments can cause problems. For example, using his telescope, Galileo found that there were mountains on the moon. This contrasted with the received tradition that the heavenly bodies were perfect spheres. However, this is not simply a triumph of evidence over philosophical theory, since – from the drawings Galileo made – we know that some of his observations were wrong. Some of his 'mountains' are not there. They must have been the result of distortions in the glass of his telescope.

This is a major problem when science reveals evidence, for the methods and equipment used in science may themselves influence what is seen. To understand something, one must take into account the method and equipment used. Nothing is ever as certain as it appears. One cannot strictly speaking say that Galileo's image of the moon's surface was a true one, although, for the purpose of looking at the earlier theory of the heavenly bodies being perfect spheres, it was more than adequate.

As we shall see, the recognition that we cannot simply observe and describe came to the fore in the 20th century, particularly in terms of sub-atomic physics. It seemed impossible to disentangle what was seen from the action of seeing it.

The problem of induction

The rise of science was characterized by a new seriousness with which evidence was gathered and examined in order to frame general theories. This approach, championed by Francis Bacon and others, became the basis of what we tend to think of as the

Newtonian world of science. The task of sifting and evaluating evidence is also reflected in the empiricism of Hume (see page 46), who challenged the certainty of its results. His argument, which is of great significance for the philosophy of science, is that all such arguments can yield at best only a high degree of probability, never absolute certainty. This process – which is termed 'inductive inference' – is the attempt to move from singular statements (i.e. statements about particular things) to general or universal statements about the world, which could take the form of 'laws of nature'. It was this inductive form of argument that distinguished 'modern' science from what had gone before.

Bertrand Russell described the 'principle of induction' by saying that the more two things were observed together, the more it is assumed that they are causally linked. If I perform an experiment only once, I may be uncertain of its results. If I perform it 100 times, with the same result each time, I become convinced that I will obtain that result every time I perform it. Thus far, it sounds no more than common sense, but it raises many problems – for it is one thing to anticipate the likely outcome of an experiment on the basis of past experience, quite another to say that the past experience proves that a certain result will always be obtained.

The inductive method

The inductive approach to knowledge is based on the impartial gathering of evidence or the setting up of appropriate experiments, such that the resulting information can be examined and conclusions drawn from it. It assumes that the person examining it will come with an open mind and that theories framed as a result of that examination will then be checked against new evidence.

In practice, the method works like this:

- Evidence is gathered, and irrelevant factors are eliminated as far as possible
- Conclusions are drawn from that evidence, which lead to the framing of a hypothesis
- Experiments are devised to test out the hypothesis, by seeing if it can correctly predict the results of those experiments.

- If necessary, the hypothesis is modified to take into account the results of those later experiments
- A general theory is framed from the hypothesis and its related experimental data
- That theory is then used to make predictions, on the basis of which it can be either confirmed or disproved.

EXAMPLE

The final step in this process is well illustrated by the key prediction that confirmed Einstein's theory of general relativity. Einstein argued that light would bend within a strong gravitational field and therefore that stars would appear to shift their relative positions when the light from them passed close to the Sun. This was a remarkably bold prediction to make. It could only be tested by observing the stars very close to the edge of the Sun as it passed across the sky and comparing this with their position relative to other stars once the light coming from them was no longer affected by the Sun's gravitational pull. But the only time when they could be observed so close to the Sun was during an eclipse. Teams of observers went to Africa and South America to observe an eclipse in 1919. The stars did indeed appear to shift their positions to a degree very close to Einstein's predictions, thus confirming the theory of general relativity.

It is clear that this process can yield no more than a very high degree of probability. There is always going to be the chance that some new evidence will show that the original hypothesis, upon which a theory is based, was wrong. Most likely, it is shown that the theory only applies within a limited field and that in some unusual sets of circumstances it breaks down. Even if it is never disproved, or shown to be limited in this way, a scientific theory that has been developed using this inductive method is always going to be open to the possibility of being proved wrong. Without that possibility, it is not scientific.

Scientific laws

With the development of modern science, the experimental method led to the framing of 'laws of nature'. It is important to recognize exactly what is meant by 'law' in this case. A law of nature does not have to be obeyed. A scientific law cannot dictate how things should be, it simply describes them. The law of gravity does not require that, having tripped up, I should adopt a prone position on the pavement – it simply describes the phenomenon that, having tripped, I fall.

Hence, if I trip and float upwards, I am not disobeying a law, it simply means that I am in an environment (e.g. in orbit) in which the phenomenon described by the 'law of gravity' does not apply. The 'law' cannot be 'broken' in these circumstances, only be found to be inadequate to describe what it happening.

A classic approach to empirical evidence

The philosopher **David Hume** (1711–1776) pointed out that scientific laws were only summaries of what had been experienced so far. The more evidence that confirmed them, the greater their degrees of probability, but no amount of evidence could lead to the claim of absolute certainty.

He argued that the wise man should always proportion his belief to the evidence available; the more evidence in favour of something (or balanced in favour, where there are examples to the contrary) the more likely it is to be true.

He also pointed out that, in assessing evidence, one should take into account the reliability of witnesses and whether they had a particular interest in the evidence they give. Like Francis Bacon, therefore, Hume sets out basic rules for the assessment of evidence, with the attempt to remove all subjective factors or partiality and to achieve as objective a review of evidence as is possible.

What Hume established (in his *Enquiry Concerning Human Understanding*, section 4) was that no amount of evidence could, through the logic of induction, ever establish the absolute validity of a claim. There is always scope for a counter-example, and therefore for the 'law' to fail.

This seemed to raise the most profound problems for science – since it cut away its most sure foundations in experimental method.

With hindsight, that might seem a very reasonable conclusion to draw from the process of gathering scientific evidence, but in Hume's day – when scientific method was sought as something of a replacement for Aristotle in terms of a certainty in life – it was radical. It was this apparent attack on the rational justification of scientific theories that later 'awoke' the philosopher Kant from his slumbers. He accepted the force of Hume's challenge, but could not bring himself to deny the towering achievements of Newton's physics, which appeared to spring from the certainty of established laws of nature. It drove Kant to the conclusion that the certainty we see in the structures of nature (time, space and causality) are there because our minds impose such categories on our experience.

In other words

Hume's challenge, set alongside the manifest success of the scientific method, led to the conclusion that the process of examining the world is one that involves the necessary limitations and structures of human reason. This is the way we see the world – and it works! That doesn't mean that we can know anything with absolute certainty; and it doesn't mean that ours is the only way of experiencing it. For Kant, we know only the world of phenomena. What things are in themselves (noumena) is hidden from us.

In many ways, this continues to be the case. I cannot know an electron as it is in itself, but only as it appears to me through the various models or images by which I try to understand things at the sub-atomic level. I may understand something in a way that is useful to me, but that does not mean that my understanding is – or can ever be – definitive.

The early 20th-century philosophical movement called **logical positivism**, whose view of language and meaning was greatly influenced by scientific method, argued for using empirical evidence as the criterion of meaning: in other words, the meaning of a statement was identical to its method of verification. It made the limitations about certainty, as suggested by Hume, the norm for all statements that were not definitions or matters of logic or mathematics (known to be true 'a priori'), but depended on evidence (therefore known to be true only 'a posteriori').

In an example in his *Problems of Philosophy* (1952), Bertrand Russell gives a characteristically clear and entertaining account of the problem of induction. Having explained that we tend to assume that what has always been experienced in the past will continue to be the case in the future, he introduces the example of the chicken which, having been fed regularly every morning, anticipates that this will continue to happen in the future. But, of course, this need not be so:

> The man who has fed the chicken every day throughout its life at last wrings its neck instead, showing that more refined views as to the uniformity of nature would have been useful to the chicken.
>
> (*op cit.* p.35)

Goodman's 'new riddle'

An important modern discussion of the problem of induction was set out by Professor Nelson Goodman of Harvard in 1954, in his influential book *Fact, Fiction and Forecast*, and the examples he gave (e.g. 'All ravens are black' and the colour 'grue' – see page 49) are frequently cited in other books.

Goodman takes Hume's view that there are no necessary connections between matters of fact. Rather, experiencing one thing following another in a regular pattern, leads us to a habit of mind, in which we see them associated and therefore to claim that one causes the other. Everything is predicted on the basis of past regularity, because regularity has established a habit.

Now, we establish general rules on the basis of particulars that we experience and those rules are then used as the basis for inference – in other words, observation of particular events lead to a rule and the rule then leads to predictions about other events. The important thing here is to realize that the past can place no logical restrictions on the future. The fact that something has not happened in the past does not mean that it cannot happen in the future.

Notice therefore that there is a circularity in the way induction is used – rules depend on particulars and the prediction of particulars depends on rules. We justify the 'rules of induction' by saying that they are framed on the basis of successful induction. That's fine for practical purposes, but it does not give any independent justification for predictions about future events. It works because it works; but that does not mean that it has to work. Goodman comments:

> A rule is amended if it yields an inference we are unwilling to accept; an inference is rejected if it violates a rule we are unwilling to reject.
>
> (4th edn, p.64)

The only justification therefore lies in the apparent agreement between rules and inferences: if a rule yields acceptable inferences, it is strengthened. The crucial question, according to Goodman, is not how you can justify a prediction, but how you can tell the difference between valid and invalid predictions.

He makes the important distinction between 'law-like' statements and accidental statements. If I use a particular example in order to support an hypothesis, that hypothesis must take the form of a general law (whether it is right or not is another matter).

To use his examples:

- I can argue from the fact that one piece of copper conducts electricity to the general principle that all copper conducts electricity.
- But I cannot argue from the fact that one man in a room is a third son to the hypothesis that every man in the room is a third son. Being a third son in this situation is just something that happens to be the case in this instance – it is not a general feature of humankind in the way that conducting electricity is a general feature of copper.

The problem of 'grue':

- All emeralds examined before time 't' are green – therefore you reach the conclusion that all emeralds are green.
- But suppose you use the term 'grue' for all things examined up to time 't' that are green and all other things that are blue.

- In this case, up to time 't', all emeralds are both green and grue; after 't' an emerald could only be grue if it was, in fact, blue.
- Now the problem is that, up to time 't', our usual approach to induction confirms 'all emeralds are green' and 'all emeralds are grue' equally – and yet we know that (after time 't') the first is going to be true and the second false. How, up to that point, can we decide between them?

In other words

From the standpoint of the inductive method, there is, prior to time 't', no way of deciding between emeralds being green and emeralds being 'grue' – both, on the evidence, are equally likely. But we know, of course, that one is very soon going to be wrong and the other right. Hence, there is a major weakness in the use of induction in order to predict what will be the case in the future.

The key feature here is that an 'accidental hypothesis' (unlike a law-like hypothesis) has some restriction in terms of time or space. In other words, it cannot be generalized. The problem with 'grue' is that it has a temporal restriction, in that it means one thing before a particular time and something else after it. The new riddle of induction is not so much Hume's problem about how you justify general laws in terms of individual cases, but how you tell those hypotheses that can correctly be projected from particular instances and those that cannot.

SUMMARY

If you want to argue from particular instances to a general law, you need to take care what features of those instances you select. Some features (like the colour of emeralds) will be general and therefore form a reasonable basis for a universal hypotheses (i.e. all emeralds are green), others will be accidental (e.g. emeralds being 'grue' or men in a room being third sons) and you cannot argue from them to a generally valid hypothesis.

Let us take a final example: 'All planets with water flowing on their surface are likely to support life.'

- We know, in the case of Earth, that it is correct. But is that a general feature of planets of a certain size and distance from their suns, or is it simply an accidental feature of our own planet?
- The big issue is that science looks for general features and principles, which have to be abstracted out of the particulars in which we encounter them. We have encountered life on only one planet – our own. Whether that is an accident, and therefore possibly unique, or whether it is a general feature of planets of certain types, we cannot know.

A mathematical universe

It is one thing to observe nature, another to explain it, and one of the key components in the explanations given by scientists in the 17th and 18th centuries was mathematics. Galileo thought that the book of nature was written in the language of mathematics, but this was not a new idea, for **Pythagoras** (570–497BCE) had argued that everything could be given an explanation in terms of mathematics. Even the title of Newton's most famous book is *Philosophiae Naturalis Principia Mathematica* – an attempt to understand the workings of nature on mathematical principles.

Work in mathematics thus provided the background to much of the advancement of science in the 17th and 18th centuries, and figures such as Descartes, whose great quest was to find a certain basis for knowledge, was as much a mathematician as a scientist and philosopher. Not all gave mathematics a key role. Some, including Francis Bacon, thought of it as a useful tool, but were primarily concerned with experimental evidence as the starting point of knowledge, whereas mathematicians were more tempted to see certainty in generalized propositions.

Abstracting from nature

It is important to recognize the nature of mathematics and the very radical abstraction that it involves. Galileo, Descartes, Huygens and Newton all produced 'formulas'. In other words, they were seeking to create a mathematical and abstract way of summing up physical phenomena. That it should be possible for an abstract formula to correspond to nature was a fundamental assumption made by those involved in the emerging sciences. Beneath it lay the deeper assumption that the world is a predictable and ordered place. Escaping from the earlier era of crude superstition and magic, they saw themselves emerging into a world where reason and evidence would triumph. But reason, in its purest form, is seen in logic and mathematics, and it was therefore natural to expect that the world would be, in principle, comprehensible in terms of 'laws of nature' which, with mathematical precision, would determine the movement of all things.

The result of this was that the science produced in this period was not what is experienced – with all its mixtures of sensations, beauty, sounds etc. – but the abstract formulas by which such things could be understood and predicted. Phenomena were thus 'reduced' to their mathematically quantifiable components.

We have already explored this briefly in looking at John Locke's distinction between primary and secondary qualities. Fully aware that colour, sound and taste were obviously linked to the human sense organs, he called them 'secondary' qualities. The primary ones were mass, location and number – exactly those things that can be measured and considered mathematically. By the end of the 17th century, science thought of 'real' nature as silent, colourless and scentless – an interlocking network of material bodies, whose activities could be quantified, analysed and expressed in the form of scientific and mathematical laws.

Notice how abstract the very concept of number is. I see three separate objects before me and describe them as being 'three'. Yet there is nothing in the description of each of them that has the inherent quality of 'threeness'. 'Three' is a purely abstract term, used in order to sum up a particularly useful feature of that experience. Thus, if I am receiving money, it is the number on the banknote that is of prime importance, its colour or the quality of its paper is of less significance. By the same token, in a collection of green objects, a dollar bill might be quite in place, its numerical value of little significance.

Hence, 'laws of nature' or 'multiplication' are not things that exist. They are not concrete entities, but descriptions of the relationships between concepts that human beings use in order to make sense of their experience.

The key thing to remember here is that mathematics is an abstraction, not a reality. A key feature of 17th-century science was that the whole scheme of highly abstract reasoning was mistaken for reality itself. Hence it was given an 'objectivity' that led to the assumption that, once all 'laws' had been formulated, there would be nothing left to discover. With the 20th century and the recognition of the validity of different and even conflicting theories, the attempt to 'objectify' this abstraction process was recognized as limited. Once you start to mistake abstraction for reality, the whole world is reduced to mathematical controlled and determined operations.

Experiments

At several points so far we have recognized that scientific evidence comes from experiments as well as from observations. In particular, once a theory has been formulated, it is important to set about finding experiments that will either confirm or refute it.

There are two fundamentally important features of scientific experiments.

The isolation of significant variables

First of all, in an experiment, a controlled situation is created in which, as far as possible, all extraneous influences are eliminated. The more delicate the thing that the experiment is to measure, the more stringent are the safeguards to eliminate external factors. Thus, for example, the experiment to test the presence of the most elusive neutrinos passing through the Earth, was conducted using a tank of absolutely pure water buried deep below the surface of the Earth, far from all possible sources of interference.

A controlled situation allows a scientist to measure just a few significant variables, eliminating all others. This generally results in a mathematical formula which relates one factor to another, enabling a general statement to be made.

To illustrate the importance of this, let us take as an example the experimental testing of a new drug. Suppose only those patients who are most seriously ill are given the new drug and those with a milder condition are given more conventional treatment. The results might well show that, statistically, more people die after taking the new drug. This would not be a valid experiment, however, because there is the obvious intrusion of an unwanted variable – namely the severity of the illness experienced by the subjects. In order for the experiment to be accurate, it would be necessary to make sure that two groups of patients were identified, each having the same mix in terms of age, sex and severity of illness. One group could then be given the new drug and the other would receive either no drug at all or some more conventional treatment.

The result of that experiment might be to say that the new drug produced X per cent increase in life expectancy. In other words, all other things being equal, this is the benefit of the drug. If it is subsequently found that there were all sorts of other factors of which those conducting the experiment were unaware, then the value of the experiment would be severely reduced.

The ability to reproduce results

If something is observed just once, it could be a freak occurrence, caused by a unique combination of circumstances. It would certainly not be an adequate basis on which to frame a scientific hypothesis. The importance of carefully defined experiments is that they enable other people to reproduce them and thus confirm or challenge their findings. Once the result of an experiment is published, scientists in the same area of research all over the world attempt to reproduce it in order to see if they get the same results or to check whether all extraneous variables have in fact been eliminated. If the results cannot be reproduced, they are regarded as highly suspect.

Comment

Notice what an important part the devising of suitable experiments plays in the overall activity of science. Planning and organizing an experiment, creating the right conditions and devising and refining measuring equipment, checking that all other variables have been eliminated – these very often constitute the bulk of the work done in modern science, compared with which the actual running of the experiment may be relatively easy.

What counts as science?

> Blind commitment to a theory is not an intellectual virtue: it is an intellectual crime.
>
> (Imre Lakatos, 1973)

Science always requires a healthy measure of scepticism, a willingness to re-examine views in the light of new evidence and to strive for theories that depend on external facts that can be checked, rather than on the mind of the person framing them. As we saw earlier, it was the quest for objectivity, loyalty to the experimental method and a willingness to set aside established ideas in favour of reason and evidence, that characterized the work of Bacon and others. There were disagreements about the extent to which certainty was possible and some (e.g. Newton) were willing to accept 'practical certainty' even though recognizing that 'absolute certainty' was never going to be possible.

In the 20th century there was considerable debate about the process by which inadequacies in a theory are examined, as we shall see in the next chapter, and the point at which the theory should be discarded. No scientific theory can be expected to last for all time. Theories may be falsified by new and contrary evidence (Popper) or be displaced when there is a general shift in the matrix of views in which they are embedded (Kuhn), and theories are seen as part of ongoing research programmes (Lakatos) based on problem solving.

On this basis, we cannot say that genuine science is what is proved true for all time, whereas pseudo-science has been (or will be) proved false. After all, something that is believed for all the wrong reasons may eventually be proved correct and the most cherished theories in science can be displaced by others that are more effective. What distinguished science from pseudo-science is to do with the nature of the claims that each makes and the methods each uses to establish them.

One feature of modern philosophy of science that reflects this is probability theory (see page 113). The improbable is more significant than the probable. Thus, if an improbable event is predicted by a theory, and proves to be the case, then the theory is greatly strengthen by it. By way of contrast, something that is quite normal and expected to happen anyway, is unlikely to be considered strong evidence in favour of a theory which predicted it.

In other words, for genuine science, there is always the attempt to balance the likelihood of something being the case against the other possibilities.

EXAMPLE

If a person persists with the infuriating habit of claiming absolutely everything that he or she does as a great success, even if to the external observer it may appear a bit of a disaster, one might well ask 'What would have to happen for it to be described as a failure?' If absolutely nothing counts as a failure, then nothing merits the title 'success' either – both are rendered meaningless in terms of an objective or scientific approach, the claim of success simply reflecting the choice to see everything in that positive way.

The claim to be scientific rests on the methods used in setting up appropriate experiments or in gathering relevant evidence and also on the willingness to submit the results to scrutiny and to accept the possibility that they may be interpreted in more than one way. The distinction between science and pseudo-science is therefore essentially one of method, rather than content.

A common feature of pseudo-science is the use of analogies or resemblances to suggest causal connections, but without being able to specify or give direct evidence for them. Two popular examples illustrate this. It has been suggested that the red colour of the planet

Mars resembles blood and that the planet should therefore be associated with the coming of war and bloodshed. What is not clear is how that planet's colour could have any possible connection with warlike tendencies among human beings on Earth. The other example, which requires absolutely no further explanation, is the traditional use of powdered rhinoceros horn as a cure for male impotence!

EXAMPLES

The most obvious example of a pseudo-science is astrology. Astronomy is regarded as a science because it is based on observations and any claims made today may need to be replaced due to further observations in the future. Astrology, however, is not considered a science, because it is based on a mythological scheme with an annual cycle of 'signs'. There is nothing that one might observe that could lead to the suggestion that Gemini should no longer rule those born in May; or that the stars should be looked at in different ways, giving different star signs. Astrologers may be meticulous in their calculations and intuitively skilled in the application of their theories to individual situations. Astrology may even be shown to be of value to the people who practise it. But neither fact (if proved true) would even start to make astrology a science. For that to happen, it would be necessary to find evidence for an objective relationship between dates of birth and general behavioural tendencies; evidence which is open to scrutiny and which can genuinely put the basis of astrology at risk.

Another example of pseudo-science is crystal therapy. The rationale given for having crystals about one's person or under the pillow at night is that they somehow have a 'vibration' that can influence moods. When challenged, the person convinced of his theory might argue that having a vibration is not limited to crystals, but is a universal phenomenon. That may be fine as a scientific theory, it sounds scientific in that it uses language associated with science, yet this does not make any serious connection between general theories about atoms and their behaviour and how you might feel calm and get a good night's sleep. Unless a theory for such a connection could be put forward in a way that was open to examination, with the possibility that it might be proved wrong, then you do not have genuine science.

It's not that it's *im*possible for you to be affected by the date and time of your birth, neither is it absolutely impossible for the crystal beneath your pillow to induce calmness – it's just that there is little objective evidence that could ever be brought to bear on either question.

The issue about what constitutes science or pseudo-science is not always straightforward. Take the example of Marxism. Clearly, Marxist theory is based on logic and the observation of the way in which society is organized and changes. In this sense, following the inductive method, Marxism might be called a science. But a Marxist is going to use his theory to interpret every event and its result – whatever happens, Marxism appears to be able to rationalize it. The same could apply to those who use Freud's theories in psychology.

This creates a problem. We shall see in the next chapter that a particular feature of scientific theories is that it should be possible, in theory, to falsify them. If they cannot be falsified – in other words, if there is no possible evidence that could ever prove them wrong – they are deemed worthless. This is because theories are used to predict events and if they argue that absolutely anything is predictable, then they have nothing to contribute. This was the basis of Karl Popper's criticism of both Marxist and Freudian thinking, arguing that an irrefutable theory cannot be scientific.

Comment

In the next chapter we shall be looking at the work of Kuhn, and particularly his view of **paradigms** and their overthrow. What is clear is that it is a mark of genuine science that problems with a theory are taken seriously and that, once those problems become overwhelming, an overall paradigm may need to be set aside in favour of one that succeeds in answering those problems. Thus his view of science is of periods of stability, punctuated by revolutions. A major feature of those approaches, which we would not call scientific, is that they are not open to the possibility of such revolutionary changes. If nothing is capable of changing one's view, then that view is not scientific.

But this should not be taken as a pejorative comment, as though only scientific views were worthwhile. There are many areas of life, for example in religion, art or relationships, in which it is perfectly valid to have a commitment and a particular chosen view which is not dependent on evidence. We simply need to accept that such things are not scientific and we should not attempt to justify them on a scientific basis.

3 THEORIES, LAWS AND PROGRESS

In the last chapter we examined the inductive method of reasoning that was basic to the establishment of modern science. We saw, however, that it presented various problems – both those recognized by Hume and those highlighted by Goodman with his problem of 'grue'. The process by which laws of nature were established and revised was far from straightforward.

During the second half of the 20th century, there was considerable debate about how science makes progress, how one law or set of laws comes to replace another and whether one can ever decide that one particular theory is inherently better than another, and, if so, on what criteria it could be judged 'better'.

In this chapter we shall look at various approaches to the way in which laws are refuted or replaced, and how science makes progress. It is particularly important to recognize something of the work of Popper and Kuhn in this area, but we shall also look briefly at Feyerabend and Lakatos. Two closely related questions are of such importance that they will not be considered here, but have chapters of their own: the issues of scientific realism and of relativism and objectivity. In examining them we shall need to cover similar ground, but with those specific questions in mind.

But before looking at the general approach taken in the second half of the 20th century, it is important to appreciate what has been called the 'received view' of scientific laws, a view which forms the background of much modern debate in the philosophy of science.

Background

Towards the end of the 19th century, the general view of science – which had built up since the acceptance of the Newtonian world-view and all that developed from it – was of a mechanistic and materialistic system. The world was thought of as being quite independent of the person perceiving it, with laws that determined its operations and the interaction of all its parts. Science was quite able to set aside all metaphysical speculation and would eventually achieve a full and systematic knowledge of the physical world. The world was a mechanism in motion, waiting for man to measure and calculate its operation. There were to be no a priori elements in scientific knowledge, all presuppositions could be set aside. The scientist was required to take an objective look at matter and formulate theories to explain its operations. The 19th-century philosopher **Ludwig Buchner** could claim without fear of contradiction that: 'There is no force without matter; no matter without force.' **Ernst Haeckel** was confident that science had already revealed almost all there was to know about the world and had displaced the crude superstitions of earlier days.

But alongside this very confident view, another was developing that eventually came to dominate scientific thinking in the early 20th century. Immanuel Kant, the 18th century German idealist philosopher, had argued that there was an absolute distinction to be made between things in themselves (noumena) and things as we perceive them to be (phenomena). All the evidence we receive from our senses is 'phenomena'; we only know what we perceive. We may assume that there is a separate reality 'out there' causing us to have those sensations, but, if so, we can never engage it directly.

Thus, from the work of **Helmholtz** in the 1870s through to **Cassirer** in the early years of the 20th century, there is the recognition that science is not looking at things in themselves, but at the structures of phenomena. In other words, science looks at the way in which we perceive the world.

The philosopher and logician **Ernst Mach** (in *The Analysis of Sensations*, 1886) argued that science reflects the content of the consciousness, as it is produced by sensation. There are no predetermined structures, but everything should be reducible to statements about sensations. The only exception to this was his acceptance of logical and mathematical propositions. So, from his perspective, a scientific theory was the description of some regularity within the phenomena of sensations.

The logical positivists

Into this situation there came the logical positivists of the Vienna Circle, of whom probably the best known are Schlick and Carnap. They were generally scientists and mathematicians, influenced by the work of the early Wittgenstein and also Bertrand Russell. They believed that the task of philosophy was to determine what constituted valid propositions. They wanted to define **correspondence rules**, by which the words we use relate to observations. They also wanted to reduce general and theoretical terms (e.g. mass or force) to those things that could be perceived. In other words, the 'mass' of a body is defined in terms of measurements that can be made of it.

In general, the position adopted by the logical positivists was that the meaning of a statement was its method of verification. If I say that something is green, I actually mean that, if you go and see it, *you* will see that it is green. If you cannot say what would count for or against a proposition, or how you could verify it through sense experience, then that proposition is meaningless.

Now, clearly, this is mainly concerned with the use of language. But for science it had a particular importance, which enabled it to dominate the first half of the 20th century. Basically, it was assumed that the process of induction, by which general statements were confirmed by experimental evidence, was the correct and only way to do science.

That seemed a logical development of the scientific method, as it had developed since the 17th century, but it produced problems. What do you do if faced with two alternative theories to explain a phenomenon? Can they both be right? Can everything science wants to say be reduced to sensations? Once a law is accepted and established, it seems inconceivable that it would simply be proved wrong. To make progress, laws that apply to a limited range of phenomena can be enlarged in order to take into account some wider set of conditions. Scientific theories are therefore not discarded, but become limited parts of a greater whole.

In other words

There were two general trends by the end of the 19th century:

1 To see the world as a mechanism, upon which science reflected and produced theories about how it worked.

2 To recognize that all our knowledge comes through the senses and that the task of science is to systematize the phenomena of sensation. We cannot know things in themselves, separate from our experience of them.

- The logical positivists argued that the meaning of a statement (scientific or otherwise) was the method by which it could be verified. Everything depended on sense experience. All theoretical terms had to show a correspondence with observations.
- Discussions about the inductive method in science should be seen against this positivist background – the narrow and precise view of language that they espoused matched what they saw as the ideal of scientific language – the means of summarizing perceptions.

But even while this view was dominating the philosophy of science, the actual practice of science – especially in the fields of relativity and quantum physics – was producing ideas that did not fit this narrow schema.

Some of the important thinking about scientific theories and how they develop and get replaced was essentially a reaction against this accepted view. We shall now turn to the work of Popper, who criticized logical positivism and showed the role of falsification in the examination and replacement of theories. But more significantly, there was a sense (as exemplified in the work of Kuhn) to see scientific theories as being framed within an overall view of the world (a *Weltanschauung*), and that radical change could take place only when one whole set of views was finally found to be inadequate and replaced by another.

Falsification

Karl Popper (1902–1994), was a philosopher from Vienna who, following some years in New Zealand, settled in London in 1945, where he became Professor of Logic and Scientific Method at the London School of Economics. He made significant contributions to political philosophy as well as the philosophy of science.

Popper's theory of falsification, although important for the philosophy of science, has much wider application. In the 1920s and 1930s, logical positivists were arguing that statements only had meaning if they could be verified by sense data. In other words, if you could not give any evidence for a statement, or say what would count for or against it, then it was meaningless. (The exception, of course, being statements of logic or mathematics, where the meaning is already contained within the definition of the words used. You don't have to go out and point to things in order to show that 2 + 2 = 4.)

In *The Logic of Scientific Discovery* (1934, translated in 1959) Popper argued that one could not prove a scientific theory to be true simply by adding new confirming evidence. Contrariwise, if some piece of sound evidence goes against a theory, that may be enough to show that the theory is false.

He therefore pointed out that a scientific theory could not be compatible with all possible evidence. If it is to be scientific, then it must be possible, in theory, for it to be falsified. In practice, of course, a theory is not automatically discarded as soon as one piece of contrary evidence is produced, because it might be equally possible that the evidence is at fault. As with all experimental evidence, a scientist tries to reproduce this contrary evidence, to show that it was not a freak result, but a genuine indication of something for which the original theory cannot account.

Comment

His attack was aimed particularly at those disciplines which he regarded as bogus rather than genuinely scientific. He was particularly critical of Marxism and Freudian psychology. He observed that Marxists have the habit of interpreting every event in terms of Marxist theory and then using such interpretations in order to confirm that theory. He argued that if nothing were allowed to falsify the Marxist view of dialectical materialism that theory could not be genuinely scientific. Similarly, he suggested that a psychologist might be tempted to give a particular interpretation of a patient's condition based on the accepted theory and to attempt to explain away or ignore anything which does not appear to fit the expectations of that same theory.

At the same time, scientists are likely to consider any alternative theories that can account for both the originally confirming evidence and the new, conflicting evidence as well. In other words, progress comes by way of finding the limitations of existing scientific theories.

A key feature of Popper's claim here is that scientific laws always go beyond experimental data and experience. The inductive method attempted to show that, by building up a body of data, inferences can be made to give laws that are regarded as certain, rather than probable. Popper challenges this on the grounds that all sensation involves interpretation of some sort and that in any series of experiments there will be variations and whether or not such variations are taken into account is down to the presuppositions of the person conducting them. Also, of course, the number of experiments done is always finite, whereas the number of experiments not yet done is infinite. Thus inductive arguments can never achieve the absolute certainty of a piece of deductive logic.

What was essential, for Popper, was to be able to say what would falsify a claim. If nothing could be allowed to falsify it, it could not have significant content. Thus he held that all genuine scientific theories had to be logically self-consistent and also capable of falsification. No scientific theory can be compatible with all logically possible evidence. An irrefutable theory is not scientific.

EXAMPLE

Consider the weight of experimental evidence in favour of Newton's laws of physics. In terms of the conditions prevailing on Earth, one can go on confirming them. Problems with them only occur when you consider extreme situations. As we saw earlier (page 45) Einstein correctly predicted the bending of light from distant stars due to the Sun's gravitational pull, which was confirmed by observation during an eclipse. The body of evidence built up through the successful application of Newtonian physics did not preclude this crucial piece of evidence which showed the limitations of his theories.

Science thus moves forward by finding evidence that refutes a previous theory and thereby causes it to be modified or discarded.

In particular, Popper's view challenges two popular philosophical ideas:

- Locke's idea that the mind is a *tabula rasa* until it receives experience
- Wittgenstein's idea, propounded in *Tractatus*, that the task of language is to provide an image of the external world.

Instead, he saw minds as having a creative role *vis à vis* experience. In the scientific realm this means that progress is made when a person makes a creative leap to put forward an hypothesis that goes beyond what can be known through experience. It does not progress gradually by the adding up of additional information to confirm what is already known, but by moving speculatively into the unknown, and testing out hypotheses, probing their weak points and modifying them accordingly.

This view of scientific work parallels the general situation of human thought, for Popper saw all of human intelligence in terms of the constant solving of problems – that is simply the way the mind works.

In effect, the goal of science is therefore to produce statements which are high in information content and low in probability of being true (since the more information contained, the greater the chance of finding a proposition to be false), but which actually come close to the truth. If would, of course, be easy to find a statement that never need fear being refuted (e.g. 'The sun will rise tomorrow'), but it offers so little information content that it is difficult to see how it can be of much practical use.

His approach to scientific method was therefore as follows:

1. Be aware of the problem (e.g. the failure of an earlier theory).
2. Propose a solution (i.e. a new theory).
3. Deduction of testable propositions from that theory.
4. Establish a preference from among competing theories.

SUMMARY

On Popper's theory, no scientific law can ever be proved, it can, at best, be given only a high degree of probability. There must always remain the possibility that a piece of evidence will one day be found to prove it wrong.

Therefore, in terms of the results of scientific work, he observes that everything is already 'theory soaked'. Everything is a matter of using and modifying theories: the basic form of intellectual work is problem solving.

Note

For Popper, the ideal is a theory which gives the maximum amount of information and which therefore has quite a low level of probability, but which nevertheless comes close to the truth. Such a theory may eventually be refuted, but it will be extremely useful, because its content will allow many things to be deduced from it. In other words, to take the opposite extreme, a theory that says nothing about anything is not going to be proved wrong, but neither is it going to be of any use!

In general, science works by means of experiments. Results are presented along with detailed information about the experimental methods by which they were obtained. The task of those who wish to examine the results is to repeat the experiments and see if they produce identical results. Now, as it goes on, a theory is going to predict facts, some of which will be verified, some of which will not. Where it has failed to predict correctly, there is danger that the theory will therefore be falsified – that is the key to Popper's approach. However, it is not quite that simple, for both Popper and Lakatos there is the recognition that falsification and the discarding of a theory generally only takes place once there is another theory ready to take its place.

In other words, if there is another theory that can account for all that this theory can account for, and then go on to account for some situations that this theory is wrong about, then that other theory is to be preferred. Explanatory power is the ultimate criterion here. Thus it is possible that, if an experiment seems to falsify a theory, that there is something wrong with the experiment or that there is some other factor involved that was not considered before. It is not simply possible to throw out a theory at the first hint of falsification. By the same token, when that alternative theory becomes available, every occasion of falsification leads to a comparison between the two theories and the one that is confirmed more broadly is the one to be accepted.

SUMMARY

- A simplistic view of falsification is that a theory is to be discarded if it is not confirmed by experimental results.
- A more sophisticated view is that a theory is discarded if it is not confirmed by experimental results and there is an alternative theory that can account for them.
- In practice, scientists learn from the failures of theories, for it is exactly at those points where existing theories are shown to be inadequate that the impetus to find a more comprehensive theory is born.

Models and paradigms

Thomas Kuhn (1922–1996) struggled to understand how progress in science could be reconciled with either the idea of straightforward induction or with the implications of Popper's falsification approach, where a single piece of evidence was sufficient to require the rejection of a theory.

He therefore developed an alternative view, based very much on an examination of how, historically, science has actually gone about its business. In practice he saw that there had been flashes of insight, but that these were in contrast to a background of routine scientific research, building and confirming what those moments of insight have hinted at. Science did not simply get rid of theories and replace them with every conflicting piece of evidence, rather – at least for most of the time – its work was gradual and cumulative.

He recognized that the basic set of assumptions that work for science over a particular period of time remain normative – that is, most scientists just get on with the job of carrying out experiments within a set of scientific assumptions that they have inherited. As laws and theories become established within the scientific community, they are used as a basis for further research. These he termed 'paradigms'.

He therefore wanted to distinguish between 'normal science' and those moments of crisis in which the whole approach is changed in what amounts to a scientific revolution. The periods of stability are dominated by a 'paradigm', but any such paradigm is going to have some problems. There problems gradually increase until they provoke a crisis for the existing paradigm, at which time there may well be the emergence of an alternative, one that is able to deal with the problems that have caused the crisis. Once that new paradigm is accepted, science settles down once again.

This process by which paradigms are accepted during periods of 'normal science' and then set aside in crises is set out in his book *The Structure of Scientific Revolutions* (University of Chicago Press, 3rd Ed, 1996).

EXAMPLE

There are many examples of paradigms being replaced in a scientific revolution. Perhaps the most obvious was the revolution that allowed the world of Newtonian physics to replace the older Earth-centred world of Aristotle and Ptolemy. Then, with Einstein's theories of relativity, the Newtonian physics, which had served science well up to that point, gave way to a very different view of the universe.

With hindsight we can see the narrowness of vision that allowed philosophers and scientists to affirm their particular vision of the world just as the scientific community is about to go through a 'paradigm shift' in which everything is going to be reassessed. At the end of the 19th century, nobody could have dreamed of the drastic changes that would happen to science during the first half of the 20th century. But at the time, given all they knew about the world, their thoughts made perfect sense.

A particularly controversial aspect of Kuhn's theory is that he claims that there is no independent evidence by which to decide between two different paradigms. All evidence is interpreted in the light of either one or the other – there is no independent standpoint from which to view the two options available.

Note

We cannot make observations that are genuinely independent of the paradigm within which we operate – simply because those observations are shaped by the paradigm. Neither is it possible to have observations that are free from any paradigm. It is therefore only rarely that a new paradigm emerges, since for most of the time 'ordinary science' works within its given parameters. Nevertheless, when a revolutionary change of view takes place, a new paradigm can emerge, and scientific debates occur when the two different paradigms come into contact with one another, each serving as a possible basis for the interpretation of evidence.

The other thing to notice in connection with Kuhn is that theories require a measure of commitment. The inductive method (as for example put forward by Hume) might allow that with every new piece of evidence we are prepared to scrap every theory we have ever held, but in practice that is simply not the case. We work within a particular paradigm and that influences our way of examining evidence and rationalizing from it. Our whole style of thinking is influenced by our paradigm and it takes something really significant to shift or replace it.

Notice that, for Kuhn, the basis of a paradigm is not justified rationally, neither is it open to direct falsification. Since it forms the structure within which evidence is evaluated, the paradigm adapts evidence to suit itself. It takes a huge imaginative leap to get outside the paradigm within which one is working. It is therefore possible to interpret Kuhn in such a way that he is seen as a relativist, since a paradigm can be evaluated against the questions asked by a particular society at a particular time, but cannot be compared with another paradigm from another period. In other words, each paradigm has its own language, and the terms used by different paradigms may be incompatible.

Comment

The 'paradigm' phenomenon is a common feature of human thinking – there are social, religious and cultural paradigms. Within any art, it is difficult to step outside one's tradition and produce something completely different. A classical style, for example, provides a paradigm within which composers or artists were content to work for most of their time.

The triumph of imagination and creativity is to get beyond one's paradigm.

Perhaps one way of summing up Kuhn's view of science is that it comprises a great deal of routine gathering of information and enlarging of our body of knowledge, punctuated by flashes of insight, in which the whole body of information is suddenly re-examined and put into a new perspective. Those moments are his 'paradigm shifts', and between them there are the long periods of normal science.

Comment

The key issue is how you are able to maintain that science can make progress, while not being able to stand back from it and have a method of judging between paradigms. If – as Kuhn and Feyerabend says – we cannot get 'outside' a paradigm and get a truly objective view of the operations of science, then how can we ever say definitively that progress has been made or that one paradigm is inherently better than another?

Indeed, Feyerabend (in *Against Method: Outline of an Anarchistic Theory of Knowledge*, Verso, 1975) said that 'progress' is misguided and impossible – we cannot get 'true knowledge', only various ways of seeing. Hence, for Feyerabend, the choice of one theory over another may be made for all sorts of personal, cultural, aesthetic and subjective reasons. Each person is free to choose his or her own view and science cannot impose absolute or fixed criteria for what is true and what is not.

If that is the case, what sort of motivation is possible? In the 17th and 18th centuries, scientists thought that they were gradually dispelling ignorance and establishing the rule of reason. Can the same impetus be found if science is merely offering a succession of optional viewpoints? It may actually be the case, but can you seriously engage in science if you believe it to be so?

Notice also that the older inductivist approach to the scientific use of evidence and experiment tended to suggest that progress was a very slow and cumulative business. With Kuhn, we see it quite otherwise – as an erratic progress, with moments of sudden advance separated by long periods of solid work with little new to show for it. Looking at the history of science, it is clear that Kuhn has a more accurate view of the history of science than the cumulative approach, for in our outline of the history of science in Chapter 2 we noted particular periods which produced significant change.

The other thing to note is that, if we were to follow Popper's falsification approach, it is unlikely that we would ever get much by way of progress. However carefully set up, experiments seldom yield results that are completely unambiguous. Hence, for a strict falsificationist, every little bit of contrary data would require a theory to be dumped. In practice that simply does not happen. If some unusual data appear it is taken seriously, but initially there is a search to find some alternative explanation – perhaps some fault with the apparatus of the experiment. Similarly the scientist would try to repeat the experiment in exactly the same way to see if the apparently 'rogue' results were achieved again. In other words, the unusual or unexpected does not yield immediate panic and the throwing out of all existing theories, rather it is part of a general process of gathering evidence and the overall paradigm is only going to be changed if the evidence against it becomes overwhelming.

But clearly, there is some sort of progress with science, even if the paradigm is not changed in one of Kuhn's moments of revolution. One way of dealing with this is put forward by Imre Lakatos (in *Falsification and the Methodology of Scientific Research Programmes*, C.U.P., 1978). Lakatos recognized that, in practice, science made progress by way of research programmes, which were essentially problem-solving activities. It was not a matter of accepting or discarding a hypothesis upon a single piece of contrary evidence, as might be suggested by a simple application of Popper's falsifiability theory, neither was it a matter of waiting for a crisis and change of paradigm. Progress was made within science through research programmes, which set out over a period of time to devise experiments and gain new facts.

Within such a programme, one might distinguish between a 'hard core' of theories, without which the programme would not be viable and which scientists would not discard without overwhelmingly good reasons, and a 'protective belt' of supplementary theories, which could be examined and changed without totally abandoning the overall programme. Thus progress can be made by adjusting the 'protective belt'.

In practice, there is likely to be more than one research programme on the go in a field of study at any one time. Progress can therefore be made when one of these is shown to be more fruitful than the others. Competition is not simply between theories, but between whole groups of theories within each research programme.

Lakatos thus criticizes Popper for not appreciating the historical continuity of theories within research programmes, making them vulnerable to falsification in a way that does not correspond to the actual way in which scientists evaluate their work. But he also criticizes Kuhn (perhaps unfairly, as we shall see, page 103) for making changes in paradigm largely irrational affairs, produced by the choices of groups of scientists, without being able to specify why a new paradigm is superior to the one it replaces.

SUMMARY

- For Popper, theories are continually being tested and may be falsified at any time.
- For Kuhn, paradigms are not changed on the basis of reason alone, but in a moment of insight. Change is rare and sudden.
- For Lakatos, progress is made through research programmes, which allow peripheral theories to change, gradually influencing a 'hard core' of key theories for that particular programme.

The status of scientific theories

If a theory is to gain acceptance, it is important that it should be compatible with other well-established theories. If predictions made by two theories are mutually exclusive, one of them must be wrong.

EXAMPLE

In the 19th century it was believed that the Sun generated its heat from the effect of gravity crushing its mass together. In other words, the Sun was gradually shrinking, giving off heat and light as it did so. Various calculations were made about how long the Sun could go on shining and thus about its age. Towards the end of the century, Lord Kelvin (based on work done earlier by Helmholtz) came to the conclusion that the Sun and Earth must be about 24 million years old. This is sometimes referred to as the Kelvin–Helmholtz time scale.

But the problem with this was that, if Darwin were right about evolution, the Earth needed to be far older. Both theories were carefully calculated: yet one had to be wrong. If Darwin were right about the time taken for species to evolve, there had to be an alternative way in which the Sun could produce huge amounts of energy.

With Einstein's theory of relativity, a few years later, that dilemma was resolved, because it gave an alternative explanation for the long term release of energy from the sun. Of course, the Sun's fuel will not last forever – but at least the theory of relativity gave a plausible explanation for its being old enough to have allowed time for evolution on Earth.

One important feature about the acceptance given to a theory springs directly from the scientific impetus that leads to its being put forward in the first place. Theories are there to explain phenomena that do not make sense otherwise. If you have something that existing laws cannot make sense of, you tend to hunt around for an alternative theory that can do just that.

Thus progress is made through a basic process of problem solving. If existing laws cannot be used to make sense of what I experience, that presents a problem. It also leads to an **instrumentalist** view of scientific laws. In other words, a law is to be judged by what it does.

KEY POINT

The key thing to remember is that the pictures and models by which we attempt to understand natural phenomena are not 'true' or 'false' but 'adequate' or 'inadequate'. You cannot make a direct comparison between the image you use and reality. You can't, for example, look at an atom directly and then consider if your image of it – as a miniature solar system, for example – is true. If you could see it directly, you wouldn't need a model in order to understand it! Models only operate as ways of conceptualizing those things that cannot be known by direct perception.

In practice, one theory (or paradigm, even) seldom gives way immediately and obviously to another. There is frequently a period of overlap during which rival theories are compared. It is also common for a new theory to be dependent initially on an older theory or paradigm, even if it subsequently becomes independent of if.

EXAMPLE

Copernicus is generally seen as overthrowing an earlier view of the universe, but in practice he was still dependent on the physics developed by Aristotle. He, like Aristotle, thought that planetary motion should be circular (perfect) and therefore used an elaborate system of epicycles to account for the observed orbits of the planets. Only later, and particularly after Galileo, was his theory seen as marking a revolutionary move away from the earlier cosmology of Ptolemy.

Thus, at any one time, scientists may be working with a number of different theories concerning any one particular area of research, one of which may come to be seen as more adequate or comprehensive than the others. There are times when a theory does not make great progress because other work alongside it needs to be done before its significance can be appreciated.

EXAMPLE

Quantum theory was put forward by Max Planck in 1900, but its significance was not appreciated fully until after publication of the work of Einstein (from 1905) and Bohr (1913), since it seemed too much at odds with pre-Einstein physics.

Naturally, the acceptance of a theory by the scientific community does not thereby guarantee that it has the status of absolute truth. Every theory is couched in language that is shaped by the assumptions and methods of the science that produces it. However, there are other criteria by which one theory may be preferred to another. Acceptance and the ability to predict are obviously essential and the former generally comes as a result of the latter, the more its predictions are confirmed, the greater is its degree of acceptance. At the same time, where there are equally successful theories, a choice between them may be made on the ground of simplicity or elegance. In other words, if there are two theories, one extremely complex and the other simple, the tendency is to accept the simpler. This follows from **Occam's Razor** by which one should not multiply causes beyond need. The simpler theory is only set aside once it can be shown that there are cases it cannot cover.

In his book *The Essential Tension* (1977), Kuhn sets out five characteristics of a good scientific theory. They are:

- accuracy
- consistency
- scope
- simplicity
- fruitfulness.

He points out that these may well conflict with one another, between (for example) a more accurate theory and one which, in practice, is more fruitful in enabling scientists to make more predictions.

His main point (and, a way of defending himself against the criticism that his view of change is based on irrational factors) is that one scientist may prefer one theory because of certain qualities and another may – by placing emphasis on other qualities – favour another. He judges that, collectively, the scientific community comes to a common mind about which theories are better than others. This is not a simple matter of weighing evidence, but of taking all five factors into account.

The Duhem–Quine approach

So far we have looked at grounds for accepting or rejecting theories individually, grouped within a paradigm or as part of a research programme. There is, however, a line of argument that questions any attempt to divide our knowledge up in this way. It is generally known as a Duhem–Quine approach, after the physicist Pierre Duhem and the philosopher W.V. Quine.

Duhem, writing in the 1890s, argued that in order to disprove a theory, you could only do it on the basis of other theories that you held to be true. If your own theories were at fault, then your disproof would be invalid. Thus, he argued that it was a mistake to try to separate hypotheses off from one another at all, but that they should be taken all together as parts of a whole.

Quine took a similar line of approach in an important article 'The two dogmas of empiricism', written in 1951. He argued that our ideas fit together as a 'fabric', so that a change in any one of them would have an impact on all the others.

Together, these reflect an important recognition of the **holistic** nature of human knowledge and this line of thinking can be seen as influencing Kuhn's view of what happens during a period of 'normal' science and also in Lakatos' recognition of the way in which theories hold together within a research programme.

In other words

Working to understand some unusual evidence or the unexpected results of an experiment, one may suddenly come up with a new theory to explain them. A key question to ask at that point is 'How does this new theory relate to everything else I believe to be true? What other theories have to be changed to accommodate this new one?' In a sense, the Duhem–Quine approach is the recognition that you cannot make a move on the chessboard without influencing the direction of the whole game. Theories have to hang together or they become meaningless.

4 SCIENTIFIC REALISM

'Scientific realism' is the term used for the view that the objects with which science deals are separate from, and independent of, our own minds and that scientific theories are therefore true of the external, objective world.

Clearly, most people assume that this is the case. The whole point of the development of scientific method at the time of the rise of modern science, of setting up experiments and gathering impartial evidence was aimed at achieving knowledge that was free from the influence of personal interests or received tradition.

However, as has become clear in looking at the ways in which theories and paradigms are developed and replaced, things are not always straightforward. We interpret evidence in the light of existing theories. What is more, there are areas of science (e.g. particle physics) where it is acknowledged that the act of investigation itself influences what is investigated. How can that yield knowledge that is truly independent of our own minds? We also saw briefly how Kant, faced with Hume's attack on certainty, explored the idea of the mind's contribution to the interpretation of all experience.

In this chapter, we shall therefore be concerned with the nature of observation, the task and influence of language and the realist implications of a reductionist approach to science.

Reality and observation

Many apparently 'modern' issues can be traced back to the philosophy of Ancient Greece, and the issue of scientific realism is no exception. In pre-Socratic times there was a fundamental disagreement between Protagoras and Democritus. Protagoras argued that all we could know were the sensations we received. We could know nothing of what was out there causing those sensations.

Consider the statement 'I see a red ball'. That is true or false depending on whether my eyes have indeed recorded light of that wavelength forming a circular pattern on my retina. I have to infer that something outside my eye has caused that to happen, but all I actually know is that optical phenomenon. (There is an additional problem concerning interpretations. I may think that I am looking at a red ball but, on approaching it, I may see that it is, in fact, a red apple. The sensations remain the same initially, but my mind interprets them as one thing or the other.)

By contrast, Democritus insisted that 'things' existed separately from our perception of them. Of course, that is an equally logical view, since the red ball surely continues to exist if I shut my eyes. (An argument made in the 17th century by the philosopher Berkeley.)

EXAMPLE

If simple observation were the only factor in determining our knowledge of reality, then nothing at all can be more certain than the fact that the Earth is stationary. For thousands of years, humankind has observed the turning of the stars and has experienced the ground beneath its feet as a fixed point from which to observe all other movement. To accept that the Earth moves around the Sun and turns on its axis on a daily basis is to move away from simple experience, to start to interpret what is seen in the light of a theory. Against all the evidence of our senses, we 'know' that we are hurtling through space. Uninterpreted evidence is therefore an inadequate basis for any scientific theory.

The key point here is the distinction between what actually exists (ontology – the theory of what exists) and what we can know about what exists (epistemology – the theory of how we know things). Ontologically, it makes sense to say that 'things' have an existence independent of our perception of them. Epistemologically, it makes sense to say that we cannot know things except by our perception of them.

Comment

The only sensible way to resolve this dilemma is to recognize that human beings are part of nature. There are not two separate things – ourselves and the world – with the only information filtering from one to another coming through sense experiences. Rather we are part of a world, and what we call sensations are those processes by which we relate to the rest of the world around us. Sensation is communication. That's why it developed. Without the ability to see, hear, smell or taste, human beings would have starved to death! The senses are processes of communication and investigation. We only get into a muddle with this if we forget the process and look merely at the results.

The actual process of observation is complex. The idea of space and the distance between objects relies on the brain linking one thing to another; the conventional idea of time appears as we remember that some experiences have already taken place. If science depends on experience, then it is dependent on our ways of looking, thinking, recognizing and remembering. In particular, it was **Immanuel Kant** (1724–1804) who argued that when we observe something, our mind has a contribution to make to that experience. He saw space, time and causality as categories imposed on experience by the mind.

The matter becomes far more complex when we consider how modern science makes connections between what we actually see (or produce in the course of an experiment) and what we infer to be objective cause.

EXAMPLE

When a metal is heated to very high temperatures in an electric arc, it emits light that can be represented as a spectrum of lines. The pattern and sequence of those lines is always the same, wherever, for example, iron is present. Of course, this applies only to iron that is hot enough to vaporize; at lower temperatures it glows and emits light across a continuous spectrum and the lines disappear.

This means that we are able to detect metals across huge distances. We can know that a particular metal is present in a distant star, without being there to analyse it. All we need to do is look at the spectral lines produced by the light from that star. If the lines match those of light given off by iron vaporized here on Earth, the conclusion is that iron is also present in that star.

In other words, what we perceive tells us about what is 'out there', but it not identical to what is 'out there'. Reality is *inferred* from observation, not identical with it.

Something is known to be present from the trace it leaves. In this case, the presence of a vaporized metal is the best explanation for that particular set of spectral lines as the light coming from that distant source is analysed.

Clearly, our sensations are limited to objects within a narrow size and distance range. Most of what we know, therefore, we have to infer from the best explanation that science offers us for those perceptions.

Comment

Inference of this sort is neither new nor unreasonable. From early times, humans saw a movement of leaves and inferred the presence of an animal in the jungle. One key difference was that primitive humans did not stop to contemplate whether the inferred animal was real or not. Depending on its size, they would either have needed to kill and eat it or retreat quickly before it killed and ate them! In other words, their skills at observation and inference had a pragmatic function – to enable them to stay alive. In some ways, science can take the same approach: if an inferred theory works and is useful, it is provisionally accepted.

Perhaps the issue goes back to Galileo or to Descartes and the quest for absolute certainty. Like primitive humans in the jungle, we cannot afford to wait to have absolute certainty before interpreting and acting on what we observe. We therefore accept inference as a working basis for our understanding of reality.

Observation in quantum theory

According to the 'Copenhagen interpretation' of quantum theory (so called because it was developed at the Copenhagen Institute of Theoretical Physics), particular states only become determinate when we observe them. In other words, our act of observing brings reality into being.

Thus, according to quantum theory, everything is actually interrelated and nothing is determined. But in an observed universe, by the act of observation, everything is determined.

Note

In terms of scientific realism, there was a fundamental disagreement about quantum theory between Bohr and Einstein.

- For Bohr (and Heisenberg, who worked with him), the uncertainty that applies to sub-atomic particles is not just a feature of our observation, but is a fundamental feature of reality itself. It is not just that we cannot simultaneously know the position and momentum of a particle, but that the particle does not *have* these two qualities simultaneously. Thus physics is really about what we can talk about – if something cannot be observed, it cannot be part of our reality. Our observation creates the reality we are observing.
- Einstein, however, took the view that there was indeed a reality that existed prior to our observation of it. Thus a particle would indeed have a position and momentum at any instant, the only thing was that it was impossible for us to *know* both at the same time. Reality is thus prior to observation. But, of course, it remains essentially an unknown reality, since as soon as we try to observe it, we are back in Bohr's world of physics where it is determined by our observation.

Schrodinger's cat

A well-known but often misinterpreted example of the issue of whether uncertainty is a feature of reality itself (the Copenhagen approach) or merely of our observation is given in the account of 'Schrodinger's Cat'. Schrodinger was opposed to Bohr's 'Copenhagen' interpretation of quantum theory. He illustrated his point by describing a hypothetical experiment:

> Suppose one were to put a cat into a sealed box, along with a bottle of cyanide, which will be smashed by a hammer if there is any decay of a radioactive substance within the box. Is the cat alive or dead?

According to Schrodinger (and common sense), the cat is either alive or dead in the box. We cannot know which is the case without opening it and taking a look – nevertheless, the reality is that the cat is either alive or dead prior to our opening the box. According to the Copenhagen interpretation, however, the cat is neither alive nor dead *until* we open the box!

Thus Schrodinger takes a view that follows Einstein's criticism of Bohr – that uncertainly is a feature of our observation, not of reality. One way of describing the situation is to say that Bohr and Heisenberg argue for essential indeterminism, whereas Schrodinger and Einstein accept only an indeterminism of observation.

Comment

There is an absolutely fundamental philosophical dilemma here.

We cannot know 'A' without observing it using method 'X'. ('X' here is related to the nature of our senses or the apparatus we need to use in order to observe 'A'.)

All we can know is the experience 'A through X'.

We may then discover a new way of observing A – leading to the experience 'A through Y'.

But we cannot know A in a way that is independent of both X and Y, neither does it make sense to try to go for a 'lowest common denominator' between the two experiences – since everything we know about A is filtered through either X or Y. What is more, within the terms of X, Y may make no sense, and vice versa.

We either say 'A has a definite nature, but we cannot know what it is. All we can know is "A through X" and "A through Y"', or we might say 'It makes no sense to say that A has a definite nature, since it appears differently in different situations.'

There is no logical way to choose between these two statement, since there is no evidence that can help decide the matter.

Hence the Copenhagen interpretation sees observation as creating reality, whereas Einstein saw reality as something prior to our observation.

The key thing is how this leaves the task of physics. For Bohr, physics is not about external reality independent of observation – it is not about what 'is' – but about what we can talk about, and of course, we can only talk about what we can observe, which is reality encountered through the particular scientific methods we use.

There is also an important distinction (made by David Bohm and David Peat in *Science, Order and Creativity*, Routledge, 1988) between the explicate order, which is known to the senses, and the implicate order, which is a restless flow of energy in events and processes. (This would seem to have parallels with Kant's distinction between things in themselves – noumena – and things as we experience them – phenomena.)

There is an important argument in favour of the anti-realist view of scientific theories, concerning the very nature of what a theory is. Theories are generalizations, they attempt to show and to predict across a wide range of actual situations. Indeed, the experimental nature of most scientific research aims at eliminating irrelevant factors in order to be able to develop the most general theory possible.

Now in the real world (as was pointed out by Duhem and others) there are no generalities. You cannot isolate an atom from its surroundings and form a theory about it. Everything interconnects with everything else – all we have are a very large number of actual situations. Our theories can never represent any one of these, because they try to extract only generalized features. Theories deal with ideal sets of circumstances, not with actual ones.

EXAMPLE

A general theory of what a hat is, may include the most significant points – that it is worn on the head, for example. But however good that general description and however useful in distinguishing hats from other garments, it will never be the description of any one particular hat. If it were, it would apply to that one thing only.

So a theory applies to everything in general only by applying to nothing in particular.

There are limitations to the application of arguments about determination and observation – one of which is that they should not be applied at an inappropriate level. Thus, for example, according to Schrodinger, we cannot apply the principles of quantum physics to human beings; they operate at very different levels of reality. We do not experience ourselves as being determined by being observed!

But clearly, there is another way of looking at this. Human beings, once observed, are determined, even if, as observers, they are not determined. But that is exactly the point that Kant was making in terms of noumena and phenomena – it was key to his 'Copernican revolution' that our minds impose order on experience. In a sense, quantum theory does the same – it is the act of observation that imposes an either/or on the otherwise indeterminate activity of particles.

Language

We always need to keep in mind that 'facts' are statements. They are not the same thing as the information we receive through the senses – rather, they are claims that arise as a result of the way in which our minds process and interpret that information.

We all have conceptual frameworks which suggest to us how we should interpret our experience. We never come to a new experience without some sort of anticipation about what it will be like. The words we use to describe it are part of that framework. They relate this new experience to what we and other people have known in the past. They are a kind of shorthand that saves us from having to begin from scratch to describe the elements of everything we see.

So the words we use, and the facts that they express, have meanings that are already given to us by the society that shares our language. Therefore, a 'fact' is never neutral in terms of language, it is never free from all that language has become as it has developed and grown its vocabulary. Everything we see, we see 'as' something; that is a general feature of experience, but it is also the result of using language. You cannot describe something unless you can find existing words that convey something similar – and, whether those words are used literally or metaphorically, they colour and give meaning to what is described.

Language is active is shaping our experience, it is not simply a transparent medium through which experience may be communicated. Once we appreciate that, we can start to see the limitations of attempts to find an 'ideal' or scientific language – an attempt made by the logical positivists, as we shall see a little later.

The propositions of science are not derived solely from facts, although they often appear to be so. Propositions always depend on other propositions and are therefore always open to question, always fallible. We can only understand a scientific theory because the words and ideas in which it is expressed are already familiar to us. We may, of course, misunderstand a theory, if the words used to describe it mean something different to us. Ideally, both speaker and hearer should get together and the speaker point directly to the realities to which the words he or she is using refer.

Of course, much of science deals with matters that are not directly observable by human sense organs; the unaided eye cannot see an atom. So it is not possible simply to compare a scientific statement with one's own experience in order to confirm or refute it. Indeed, if that were the case, there would have been no need for science to develop experiments or equipment to extend the range of what we can detect. What we are asking, if language is somehow to be shown to reflect the reality we are trying to describe, is that there should be correspondence between that language and the reality –

and that requires some way of showing that what is being said corresponds with something that is observable. Now clearly, if you could observe something directly there would be no problem. The task of scientific language is to describe what goes beyond observation. The question is how it can be shown to do so or to what extent language is actually selected and given its validity by the subjective wishes of the person using it or by the society that creates its meanings. The major question therefore: is your language objective (accurately reflective what is 'out there') or subjective (the product of your own personal and social circumstances) or does it contain an element of both and – if so – how are they balanced?

Clarity

Clarity is a key feature in any language which is to convey scientific theories accurately. A good example of the scientific insistence on correct language is in the complaints made by Galileo about those who tried to cover over their ignorance about causation by saying that something 'influenced' or 'had an affinity with' something else. These, he believed, had no factual meaning and it would have been far more honest to say that one did not know any way in which the one could cause the other. He considered that all such vague use of language gave the impression that the speaker was pretending to offer a reason, but without any concrete evidence, and therefore had a tendency to mislead.

What then can be said about the world, and what cannot? We have already encountered the logical positivists (see pages 47 and 62). Impressed with the obvious success of the scientific method, they sought to accept as factually correct only those statements whose meaning could be verified with reference to the sort of evidence that would be appropriate in a scientific experiment. Following the work of Mach and Russell, they divided all statements up into logical and mathematical terms on one side and claims about empirical facts on the other. The former were known prior to experience (a priori) but the latter needed to be related to the objects of sense experience.

If words thus pictured the objects of sense experience, the problem was to find the correspondence rules by which one could relate a particular term to the observations upon which it was based. If you couldn't, in theory at least, specify the observations upon which something was based, then it was meaningless.

Wittgenstein had a remarkable statement at the opening of his book *Tractatus*:

> The world is everything that is the case.
>
> (*Tractatus 1*)

He took the view that the function of language was to picture the world:

> The totality of true propositions is the whole of natural science.
>
> (*Tractatus 4.11*)

He ends the work with the equally famous phrase:

> Whereof we cannot speak, thereof we must remain silent.

Now, *Tractatus* has been a hugely influential book and – as is well known – later in his life Wittgenstein was to develop a very different approach to language. But for our purposes here, apart from the fact that he saw the function of language as pointing to external facts, we need to note one absolutely crucial thing: that science is to do with propositions, not with external 'things'.

In other words

Science does not make the atom what it is or create DNA or shape the universe from the 'Big Bang' onwards. Science is not the same thing as the world it investigates. It is – exactly as Wittgenstein said – the totality of propositions. (I omit his reference to 'true' because many scientific propositions are known to be false, or may one day be shown to be false.) But the fact remains that 'science' is a network of words, ideas, mathematical calculations, formulas and theories. It is a form of language. It is a human construct. That is why it is both possible and important to have a philosophy of science, for once investigations and experiments are carried out, their results are evaluated and find their place within this ever-changing network of propositions. Without thought and language, science does not exist. Philosophy can remind scientists that facts always contain an element of interpretation. Facts are the product of a thinking mind encountering external evidence and they therefore contain both that evidence and the mental framework by means of which it has been apprehended and through which it is articulated.

Correspondence

The clear implication of the whole approach of the logical positivists was that the language of science should simply offer a convenient summary of what could be investigated directly. In other words, a scientific theory is simply a convenient way of saying that if you observe a 'particular' thing on every occasion that these 'particular' conditions occur, then you will observe this 'particular' phenomenon. What scientific statements do is to replace the 'particulars' of experience with a general summary.

Clearly, the ultimate test of a statement is therefore the experimental evidence upon which it is based. Words have to correspond to external experienced facts.

The problem is that you can say, for example, that a mass or a force is measured in a particular way. That measurement gives justification for saying that the terms 'mass' or 'force' have meaning. But clearly you cannot go out and measure the mass of everything, or the totality of forces that are operating in the universe. Hence such general terms always go beyond the totality of actual observations on which they are based. They sum up and predict observations.

For the logical positivists, the truth of a statement depended in being able (at least in theory) to check it against evidence for the physical reality to which it corresponds. Scientific theories can never be fully checked out in this way, since they always go beyond the evidence; that is their purpose, to give general statements that go beyond what can be said through description.

Dispositional properties

When a material is described, it is necessary to say more than what it looks like; one needs to say (based on experiments) how it is likely to behave in particular circumstances. Thus, if I pick up a delicate piece of glassware, I know that it has the dispositional property to be fragile. The only meaning I can give to that property is that, were I to drop the glassware, it would break.

Now the term 'fragile' is not a physical thing; it is an adjective rather than a noun. I cannot point and say 'there is fragile'. I use the word 'fragile' as a convenient way of summarizing the experience of seeing things dropped or otherwise damaged. It is thus possible to have general terms which are meaningful and which satisfy the requirement of logical positivism that the meaning of a statement is its method of verification. It would be easy (but expensive!) to verify that all glassware is fragile.

Interpretation

Paul Feyerabend (1924–1994) pointed out that we are constantly interpreting experience and that our interpretation is linked to all the rest of our experience. Whatever I come across, I interpret. Interpreting is part of the process of observation.

EXAMPLE

I look into the sky and see a small black dot. The fact that I see that dot is neither true nor false, it is simply a fact. If I go on to say 'There's a plane' it might be true, on the other hand, if the dot turns out to be a bird, then my statement is false.

The logical positivists had argued that, in order to show that something is correct, I must be able to show ways in which that statement corresponds to external reality. I need to specify my evidence. Feyerabend argued that this is, in principle, impossible, since the evidence I produce is again part of my interpretation of the world. I cannot get outside that interpretation.

The result of this is that one cannot 'fit' one's statements and interpretations to the world itself. One cannot say that they are either true or false in an objective way, so, for Feyerabend, there is no 'truth' in science.

Different people have different ways on interpreting experience. Each has an overall *Weltanschauung* ('world-view'). The problem is that there is no way of judging between different world-views, there is no way of getting beyond them and comparing them with some objective (uninterpreted) reality.

Comment

In a way, this dilemma of not being able to get outside one's own interpretation, is rather like the problem Kant had in the 18th century with the difference between things in themselves (noumena) and things as we perceive them to be (phenomena). We simply can't get around phenomena, because our ways of knowing are dependent upon them. We cannot get a view of the world that is from nowhere, as every view is from somewhere and that 'somewhere' determines how the world is seen.

Fine, but at the end of the day, we have to get things done. There need to be ways of assessing one view as more valuable than another, even if we cannot say that one is right and the other wrong. We shall explore this further in Chapter 5.

Reductionism and its implications

We saw earlier that Wittgenstein and the logical positivists aimed to assess all language in terms of the external reality to which it pointed and to judge it meaningful if, and only if, it could be verified by reference to some experience. In other words, to say 'My car is in front of the house' means 'If you go and look in front of the house, you will see my car'. If a statement could not be verified (at least in theory), then it was meaningless. The only exceptions to this were statements about logic and mathematics, which were true by definition, and generally termed '**analytic statements**'.

Logical positivists believed that all '**synthetic statements**' (i.e. those true with reference to matters of fact, rather than definition) could be 'reduced' to basic statements about sense experience.

Reductionism is the term we use for this process. It 'reduces' language to strings of simple claims about sense experience. However complex a statement may be, in the end it comes down to such pieces of sense data, strung together with connectives (e.g. if this... then that...; and; but; either / or). It was one of the two 'dogmas of empiricism' attacked by Quine (see page 78).

Now reductionism is primarily about language, but how we deal with language reflects our understanding of reality. So reductionism influences the approach that we take to complex entities and events.

There are two ways of examining these:

- A **reductionist** approach sees 'reality' in the smallest component parts of any complex entity (e.g. you are 'nothing but' the atoms of which you are made up).
- A holistic view examines the reality of the complex entity itself, rather than in its parts (e.g. you understand a game of chess in terms of overall strategy, rather than the way in which individual pieces are being moved).

Science can operate in both ways. On the one hand, it can analyse complex entities into their constitutive parts and, on the other, it can explore how individual things work together in ways that depend on their complex patterning.

EXAMPLE

In the early days of computing, every command had to be learned and typed in order to get a program to work. In basic word processing, one needed to remember the code for 'bold' for example and enter that before and after the word to be emboldened in the text. In a modern word processor, one simply highlights the text and clicks on a button labelled 'bold'. The more complex the processor, the simpler the action required.

We all know that, beneath the apparently instinctive operations of programs, there is a level of code in which everything is reduced to simple bits of information in the form of '0's and '1's. The letter you have typed, or design you have drawn is 'nothing but' those bits of information – there is nothing in the computer memory to represent it other than that such strings of machine code. Yet what you see in the design you have drawn, or mean by what you have written, is of a different order of significance from the basic code into which the computer reduces it.

In theory, a perfectly programmed computer would respond

automatically and one need never be aware of the program, the commands or the machine code. One would simply express oneself and it would happen – the software would have become transparent.

Perhaps that is what happens with the human brain. It is so complex that there is no opportunity to examine the firing of individual neurones – it just 'thinks'. That does not mean that the thinking takes place in some other location – that there is some secret 'ghostly' mind that does the thinking – simply that the process is so complex that it is experienced as spontaneous. In this perspective, reductionism is true but irrelevant. Things can be reduced to that basic level, but who needs to do so? The question is not rhetorical and has a clear answer. Research into the effects of strokes and the ability of patients to recover from them has shown that specific portions of the brain have very specialized functions. Although speech, sight or the ability to move one's arms are not experienced as neurone activity in a particular part of the brain, that is what they are in a 'reductionist' analysis – and knowing that can lead to a better understanding and treatment.

Various issues will be raised later that are influenced by the reductionist approach. One is the issue of freedom and determinism – since what is experienced as holistically free can be seen on a reductionist analysis as determined. Chaos and complexity issues are also relevant here, as are many aspects of the social sciences.

Within the overall scope of science, reductionism has been fundamentally important, since it was the emphasis on evidence as the basis for knowledge that led to the development of modern science. The whole empirical approach to knowledge implies a measure of reductionism. Contrariwise, as we have seen, it is not the only kind of understanding that science uses, and that there are occasions when complex entities need to be considered from the perspective of their complexity, rather than their constituent parts.

5 RELATIVISM, INSTRUMENTALISM AND RELEVANCE

From time to time philosophers have sought a point of absolute certainty, from which to build up the edifice of human knowledge. Probably the most famous example was Descartes, who was determined to doubt everything possible in order to find the one indubitable statement (which was, of course, his famous 'I think, therefore I am'). This craving for clear-cut, unambiguous language can be found in David Hume, for example, who wanted to cut away all metaphysical nonsense and base his understanding on sense experience. The logical positivists too, with their background in science, wanted a form of language that would allow no scope for metaphysics or for anything that could not be evidenced through the senses.

Sadly perhaps, we have already seen that such a hope is illusory. Phenomena may be interpreted in a variety of ways. A key question for the philosophy of science therefore is this: How can I decide between alternative theories?

In this chapter, we shall start by looking at the theory-laden nature of all scientific observations and the dilemma of how one decides between them. Then we move on to 'instrumentalism' as a way of making just such a choice and also look at relevance as a criterion for deciding between theories.

Theory-laden observations

We saw in Chapter 2 that the process of induction is based on the idea that it is possible to get information about the world which is independent of the person who gathers it. Francis Bacon insisted that a scientist should set aside all personal preferences in assessing data, in the hope that any theory derived from them should equally apply to other observers and other times.

But can we actually observe nature without in some way influencing it by our observations? If we cannot, then we must accept that much of what we think of as evidence is, in fact, shaped and selected by our own mind.

Sometimes, observations in one area of experience can lead to a general theory in another. For example, Darwin is best known, of course, for his theory of natural selection. However, in *Origin of Species*, before putting forward his theory of natural selection, he considered the way in which humans breed animals and plants. He observed the deliberate interference in the normal reproductive process in order to enhance or eliminate certain features. Through these observations, he was led to ask what factors in the wild might operate to bring about the same progressive changes that humankind are able to generate artificially. He saw this in the competitive struggle for existence in a situation of finite resources (as in the work of Malthus) and thence to the theory of natural selection.

As he presents his argument, Darwin moves from the observation of selective breeding towards his general theory of natural selection. Now, in terms of the process of gathering the evidence that led up to his formulation of the theory of natural selection, did Darwin have the model of domestic selective breeding in mind? If so, was it conscious? And whether conscious or not, did it influence the way in which he observed, gathered and presented evidence for his theory?

Looking at the *Origin of Species*, we can see the way in which Darwin moves from observations, to the framing of models to account for them, to an overall theory. We can also trace ideas that influenced him (e.g. Malthus and Lamark). The overall effect is to recognize that Darwin did not come to observe creatures on the Galapagos Islands with a completely blank mind, devoid of theories. As he observed them, he must have been constantly thinking through his fund of existing knowledge for some explanation for what he saw. The detailed records he made showed what he considered to be significant.

The general point that this illustrates is of fundamental importance for science. Observations and evidence are not free from the influence of theories. We examine things with some purpose and therefore some idea in mind.

Comment

This conclusion has, in part, been forced upon the scientific community by the impact of relativity and quantum theory, neither of which is easy to square with the view that there is a single, objective truth to be had.

In quantum theory there is a new relationship between observer and observed. The world cannot be divided between independent, objective things and human observers. We influence whatever we observe. Bohr and Heisenberg showed that we can no longer describe something at the sub-atomic level in a way that is independent of our act of observation. In quantum theory it really made no sense to think in terms of getting 'outside' our process of observation to see what is 'really' there; the answers we get depend on the questions we ask.

Clearly, the scientist (or anyone else, for that matter) cannot be a sufficiently detached observer that his or her habitual way of looking at the world does not influence how things are seen.

Two thinkers whose names come up frequently in this context are Kuhn and Feyerabend. Kuhn pointed out that the paradigm within which science works during periods of 'normal' science is a powerful factor in shaping the way in which scientists work, and it is not scrapped the moment contrary evidence is found. Equally, he pointed to the difficulty in comparing paradigms, simply because as all evidence is interpreted either in the light of the one or the other, it cannot be free of all influences. Feyerabend takes a rather more radical line, arguing that there may be any number of competing views, without any way, in principle, of deciding between them.

Of course, scientists do not work alone. Karl Popper argued that science was not subjective, in the sense of being the product of a single human mind, but neither could it be strictly speaking objective, since it is not made up of uninterpreted experience. Rather, he argued that science transcends the ideas of individuals and is to be understood mainly in terms of the understanding of the whole scientific community. This idea is found also in the work of Lakatos, who speaks of theories being developed within 'research projects' rather than in isolation. It also reflects Kuhn's position that paradigms are changed as a result of an overall consensus within the scientific community.

Alternative models

Earlier, when looking at falsification, we saw that more sophisticated approaches to falsification allowed that a theory would be discarded only when an alternative was found that could account for whatever evidence suggested that the first theory was inadequate. In other words, a process of scientific enquiry should be constantly looking to see if there are alternative theories to account for the evidence to hand – the existing theory is then rejected if another emerges that is more comprehensive.

EXAMPLE

There is nothing wrong with Newtonian physics if your interests are limited to basic mechanical devices on the surface of this planet. In extreme situations, however, one needs to move from Newton to Einstein. Newtonian physics is therefore seen as limited rather than wrong. Einstein's theories of relativity are preferred simply because they can predict events that are beyond the scope of Newton.

Radically different theories may be equally compatible with the evidence. How then do you choose between them? One criterion might be the degree to which they can 'fit' existing evidence and theories. Thus, for Kuhn, during periods of 'normal science' new theories tend to conform to the existing paradigm.

Alongside conformity to existing theories, a new theory may be examined in terms of its inherent simplicity and elegance. As we saw earlier (page 77), Kuhn thinks that there are five different qualities to be taken into consideration.

Yet this should not detract us from recognizing the serious problems caused by the variety of possible interpretations. Quine argued that theories are so underdetermined by data that is it possible to hold whichever of them you choose, and this line is taken also by Lakatos and Feyerabend. The whole problem is that evidence alone is not enough to decide effectively between theories – any number of which may, at any one time, be adequate interpretations of the given data. Underdetermination (the term generally used for this problem) is a major factor in supporting this relativist approach to scientific theories.

Comment

There is an interesting parallel here between the work of philosophers of science in looking at the variety of possible theories (e.g. Quine and Feyerabend) and that of philosophers of language who undertake deconstruction (e.g. Derrida). In literature, this led to the view that a text could have any number of different interpretations and that there was no definite 'meaning'. A text could mean whatever one chose it to mean, with no ultimate criterion of interpretation.

Some authors and literary theorists argue that this produces anarchy and chaos and is not in line with the intention of the author who produces the text in the first place. In the world of science, a similar complaint can be made – namely that there needs to be some way of evaluating competing theories, if any progress is to be made.

Lakatos argues that the history of science shows that different 'research programmes' work alongside one another in a competitive way and it may therefore be far from clear which of them will come to dominate.

And, of course, thinkers such as Popper and Feyerabend are happy to accept a pluralistic approach to theories competing freely with one another. Lakatos in particular thinks that it is right to work with a new theory, giving it the benefit of the doubt and shielding it from attack from more established theories, even if it is yet to yield any positive results. He takes this position, because otherwise he sees little practical opportunity for science to make progress, since a majority of new possibilities will be snuffed out before they ever get established enough to mount a serious challenge to an existing theory or paradigm. In practice, it takes a really crucial experiment, to provide the evidence to establish or refute a theory – and constructing such an experiment is a far from obvious task.

In practice, a research programme should yield both new facts, and also new theories; in other words, it should produce what amounts to a programme of continuous growth. It is not enough for a theory to have a fundamental unity and consistency. Thus, for example, Lakatos is critical of Marxism as a theory, arguing that, since 1917, Marxism had not produced any new 'facts'. In practice, he was therefore critical of any theory that had become monolithic and static. Lakatos pointed out that:

> The direction of science is determined primarily by human creative imagination and not by the universe of facts which surrounds us.
>
> (from his collected papers, published in 1978, four years after his death)

Instrumentalism

Another of Kuhn's qualities to look for in a good scientific theory is fruitfulness – the degree to which each theory is able to make accurate predictions, in other words, its usefulness as an instrument for the application of science. He argued that the main test of science is its ability to solve puzzles. If a theory does this, it is useful and is developed; if it fails, then scientists look elsewhere.

Therefore, even if we cannot decide if a theory is right, we can at least check to see what it can do for us. Indeed, we saw in the section on the inductive method (see page 44) that making and checking out predictions based on a theory is a standard way by which that theory is assessed scientifically. Theories are therefore tools for predicting; this view is referred to as the 'instrumentalist approach'.

Science tends to take a pragmatic rather than an absolute approach to truth. We cannot be certain that any of our theories are absolutely correct and we know that they will in all probability be replaced eventually by better ones. Therefore, in practice, we have to go for the most useful way of understanding the world that we have to hand, even if the theories we use already have recognizable limitations. We cannot wait for perfection.

This approach was not new. Copernicus' Sun-centred cosmology was regarded as a useful way of calculating the motion of the planets, even though it might be seen as false in itself. When, in the preface to his work by Osiander, it was claimed that the theory was merely a useful tool for helping with the calculation of planetary motion, that was exactly what we would now call an 'instrumentalist' approach to scientific theories. Indeed, given the problems faced with showing that Copernicus' views corresponded to the actual way things are, it was wise to take an instrumentalist view.

We can therefore make a distinction between understanding the role of scientific theories as 'active' or 'passive'. A passive approach would be that of traditional empiricism, whereby the theory reflects the imprint of evidence on the mind. An active approach is one in which the mind takes the evidence of the senses and works with it, putting out theories and testing them, seeking to mould experience to fit in with its previous understanding.

In philosophical terms, this active approach was put forward by Kant. He argued that the categories by which we understood experience – e.g. space, time and causality – were not in some way 'out there' in the evidence of our senses, but were imposed on our experience by the mind. They were the way the mind organized what came to it through the senses. There were also thinkers, such as the 19th-century French mathematician, physicist and philosopher Poincaré, who go a step further and see the mind as playing a more active role still, building up schemes by which we can understand the evidence we receive.

Duhem, at the beginning of the 20th century, assessed theories in instrumental terms, looking at their explanatory power. Yet he believed that we are always constructing concepts by which to grasp reality, hoping that, in the end, we will find a theory that is neutral and will reflect reality as it is in itself. Thus, even if our present assessment of theories is instrumental, there can remain a goal of some perfect theory that will explain reality in some absolute way.

Comment

Duhem's view allows for progress towards some future ideal of scientific knowledge. Perhaps that reflects the fact that he was working at the end of the 19th century and the first years of the

20th century, at a time of great optimism. However, the need to keep open the possibility of real progress is emphasized by, for example, Lakatos (who sees it as being achieved by competition between research programmes) as against the extreme relativist position of Feyerabend.

Karl Popper argued that, when you have a choice of theories to explain some phenomenon, you should opt for the one that is better corroborated than the others, is more testable and entails more true statements. In other words, you should go for the one that is most useful to your task in hand. And he says that you should do this, even if you know that the theory is actually false!

But we now need to step back from that pragmatic use of theories and ask about the implications it has for their status and function. What is clear is that theories are used, they are instruments we devise in order to understand the world. They are judged according to how effective they are in explaining what has happened or in predicting what will happen.

Thus, theories are not 'out there' waiting to be discovered. They are human creations; instruments to be used in the process of understanding the world.

Popper called theories 'instruments of thought'. They are our own inventions; highly informed guesses at explaining phenomena. They may be proved wrong – and, of course, it is central to Popper's philosophy of science that theories can always be falsified, but never fully or finally proved to be right.

Key points

1. Theories are to be seen in the context of the overall scheme of thought within which they are produced.
2. Laws are not simply true of false, but are methods of expressing regularities that have been observed. Laws are therefore instruments for drawing conclusions within an overall scheme of thought.

Relevance

Thomas Kuhn argued that a group of scientists can share a single *Weltanschauung*, and that a theory might be judged as to its relevance within that world-view and the presuppositions of the scientific community as a whole.

By the same token, Kuhn may be challenged on this, since individual scientists, even if they are presently working on the same project, are likely to have differences in background, experience and training. It is not necessary that they will therefore have an identical world-view, but will have slight variations and this may mean that one will accept a theory more readily than another.

Feyerabend goes a step further. He sees the process of putting forward new theories as a continuous one, he finds no absolute way of deciding between the theories put forward, with the danger that knowledge is reduced to the prejudices or inclinations of a particular sector of the scientific community. That a theory seems relevant to the interests of one group, does not guarantee that it will be relevant to others.

One can also argue, of course, that relevance is shown fundamentally in the ability to predict, in which case relevance as a criterion become a particular example of predictability. Lakatos speaks of science making progress through competing research programmes, in which 'thought experiments' throw up new theories, which in turn refine the questions that are being explored. A theory, for Lakatos, is examined in the light of the research programme that has developed it and is therefore judged by its relevance to that programme.

He sees research programmes as either progressive (if it can lead to predictions that are then confirmed, enabling the overall coherence of the programme to be maintained) or degenerative (if it fails to predict or loses its overall coherence). In other words, a research programme needs to show development – science cannot stand still.

Comment

You cannot always predict which lines of research will be successful. It is possible that an approach which now seems hopeless will one day be proved correct or the most reasonable approach in the light of present knowledge will be shown to be inadequate. Although Lakatos gives a useful way of distinguishing progressive from degenerative research programmes, it is far easier to do this with hindsight. What is far from clear is how one might choose between them at the time. Science is full of surprises.

The problem is that, if 'relevance theory' shows that laws and observations are to be judged by their relevance to an overall scheme of thought, this can degenerate into saying that theories should be judged by the extent to which they correspond to the particular insights and prejudices of the present scientific community. Add to this the theory that all observations are theory laden and that you are predisposed to see what you expect to see and there seems no way to compare rival theories, to reach conclusion about the relative worth of research programmes or even judge between sections of the scientific community.

Comment

The issues raised in this chapter go beyond the earlier, straightforward questions about whether theories are true or not, in that they address the way in which theories are actually used, changed or discarded within the scientific community.

Contrariwise, this could lead to the extreme view that any group of scientists can accept whatever theories they find useful, with no effective way to decide between them. Such scientific anarchy would clearly be non-productive, since it is the desire to test out and compare theories that enables science to develop. Part of the task of the philosophy of science is to relate these issues to basic questions of epistemology (theory of knowledge) and metaphysics (the fundamental structures of reality), simply because it is possible to ask whether a theory is right or wrong in a way that cannot be decided by taking a vote among scientists. Whether it is possible to find an answer or not, it is at least valid to ask if one theory is inherently better than another, given our present state of overall knowledge.

This is the position taken by F. Suppe, editor of *The Structure of Scientific Theories* (University of Illinois, 1977). Commenting on the changes that took place through the 1960s and early 1970s, he assesses the rigidity of the old positivist approaches and the extreme flexibility of Feyerabend and concludes:

> Good philosophy of science must come squarely into contact with the basic issues in epistemology and metaphysics; and the attempt to do epistemology or metaphysics without reference to science is dangerous at best.
>
> (p.728)

In other words, even if we are to consider the status of scientific theories primarily from the perspective of their usefulness and relevance within the scientific community that produces them, it is still important that they should be examined in the light of the overall philosophical questions about the nature of existence, even if no definitive answers can be given.

6 PREDICTABILITY AND DETERMINISM

Is the world simply chaotic and unpredictable or is it ordered according to physical laws that we can understand on the basis of experimental evidence? Does everything happen by chance or is it determined by causes, only some of which we may know? Are freedom and chance illusions generated by our ignorance of all the facts?

Presented starkly, such questions have implications for religion and morality as well as for science and for our general understanding of the nature of reality (metaphysics). However, as we have seen in earlier chapters, matters are not that simple.

First of all, we have seen the way in which scientific laws are produced by a process of induction, based on experimental evidence and observed facts. They may therefore be regarded as the best available interpretation of the evidence, but not as the only possible one. They do not have the absolute certainty of a logical argument, but only a degree of probability, proportional to the evidence on which they are based.

Having said that, when we look at the way in which science developed in the 17th and 18th centuries, it is clear that reason, order and predictability were at its heart. To interpret events as a matter of luck, fate or the capricious will of the gods was seen as superstition, to be set aside by the reasonable explanations of the emergent sciences.

In this chapter we shall consider the view that the world *is* predictable and, taken to its logical conclusion, that everything is determined. We shall then look at the inherent weaknesses of that view, in terms of scientific method and also in terms of those features of the world known to science which cannot be fitted into such a view – in particular the behaviour of sub-atomic particles.

We shall also need to look at the whole issue of whether it is possible to deduce laws from statistical evidence and how such general statistical laws relate to the causal or free actions of the individuals that go to make up such statistics. This, of course, is particularly appropriate in considering the social sciences.

Determinism

With the development of modern science, there came a general assumption that the world was predictable and capable of being understood rationally. This was, of course, fundamental to that whole movement in thought that we tend to refer to as the Age of Reason. As we saw in the historical introduction, the development of the physical sciences, leading up to the work of Newton, presented the world as essentially a mechanism, whose workings were understood in terms of the laws of nature.

Both English Empiricism and German Idealism agree on this fundamental predictability and determination of things. Thus Hume, as we saw in the chapter on induction, thought of an apparent chance event as merely a sign that we were unable to know all the forces operating upon it. Within the limits of the empirical method, he viewed everything as determined by physical laws. He commented:

> 'tis commonly allowed by philosophers that what the vulgar call chance is nothing but a secret and conceal'd cause.
>
> (*A Treatise of Human Nature*)

Kant, from a very different starting point, affirmed the regularity and necessity of seeing everything in the world as being causally determined. For the purposes of this argument, it is less important whether those regularities are empirically verified or imposed by the human mind, the essential thing is that there is no place for the chance occurrence or random event. Everything is either known and predictable, or is potentially so.

The classic expression of this view is given by **Pierre Laplace** (1749–1827), who held that, if one were to know all the causes operating, then, having known one single event or thing, it would be possible to demonstrate both everything that had taken place and everything that would take place. The whole universe comprised a single, predictable mechanism:

> Given for one instant an intelligence which could comprehend all the forces by which nature is animated and the respective situation of the beings who compose it – an intelligence sufficiently vast to submit these data to analysis – it would embrace in the same formula the movements of the greatest bodies of the universe and those of the lightest atom; for it, nothing would be uncertain and the future, as the past, would be present to its eyes.
>
> (*A Philosophical Essay on Probabilities,* 1816)

Now there are two different senses in which one can speak of determinism:

- the theoretical ability to account for every human choice
- the view that everything is part of a single chain of causation.

While the first is relevant for morality, the second is of principal interest for the philosophy of science.

Clearly, if we take the second of these to be the case, then what we choose to do has a profound effect on the future – since, even if we are genuinely free to choose, that choice is immediately taken up as part of the network of causes.

In other words

Choosing to turn right precludes all the events and experiences that might have taken place if one had chosen to turn left.

This allows for individual freedom, in that it does not require the future to be determined entirely by the past (the position taken by Laplace). But once it is combined with the first sense of determinism – that my choice is predictable – then it appears that freedom is either an illusion or it belongs to some order other than the physical one (in other words, mental operations are not susceptible to physical laws).

Some historical perspectives

Democritus, a Greek philosopher of the 5th century BCE, was an atomist (see page 3). He considered everything to be comprised of atoms, which could not have emerged out of nothing and which he therefore considered to be eternal. However, observing that everything in this world is subject to change and decay, he concluded that physical bodies were but the temporary gathering together of these eternal atoms and that they changed as their component atoms dispersed to form other things. He therefore considered it theoretically possible to predict how each and every thing would behave, simply because that behaviour was determined by the atoms of which it was composed.

This view was taken up by the Epicureans who saw the whole universe as a single determined mechanism, operating on impersonal laws. For them, it had important implications for human morality and self-understanding: if we are but temporary, composite creatures, with our life determined by these impersonal laws, it is perfectly valid to see the chief end in life as being the quest for happiness and well-being.

From the same period, you have a very different approach taken by the Stoics. They held that everything in the universe was ordered by a fundamental *logos* – reason or word – and that one simply had to accept what could not be changed.

Comment

From this period of Greek philosophy we seem to have two utterly different views: one that the world is constantly changing, the other that it is ordered by reason. Both, however, work on the basis that everything is predictable and that freedom is severely curtailed by the very nature of the world in which we live. In this they anticipated the later debates about determinism.

The mechanistic view of the universe given by Newtonian physics suggested that everything may be described in terms of fundamental 'laws of nature' which operate with mathematical precision. The clear implication of this is that, if all the laws were known, it would be possible to predict exactly what would happen. That was the ideal of scientific knowledge. If something unpredictable happens, it simply indicates that there is some new law of nature, of which we are unaware, operating in this situation.

Thus science came to assume that everything had a cause – or indeed a large number of causes working together – which determined exactly what it was, even if that determination could not be exhaustively demonstrated.

In other words

If everything follows laws of nature, then, even if we cannot prove that everything is determined rather than a matter of chance or personal freedom, we have to assume that it is.

How then do we account for the experience of human freedom? What does it mean to choose, in a world where everything is determined? Central to the way in which science coped with such questions was the view, put forward by **Descartes** (1596–1650), of a radical mind/body dualism. The body was extended in space and time and was controlled by the laws of nature. The mind, although linked to the body (through the pineal gland), was not extended in space and was therefore free from the determination of physical laws. It was this Cartesian dualism, along with the rise of modern science, that resulted in the perception of a mechanical universe, totally conditioned and determined, every movement theoretically predictable. Human beings could contemplate and act within such a world with apparent freedom, since their minds were not part of it – the mental realm was quite separate from the physical.

The philosopher and mathematician **Leibniz** (1646–1716) presents what amounts to a rather different angle on determinism. He argued that a change in any one individual thing in the world would require that everything else be changed as well. It might be possible for the whole world to be different, but not for the rest of the world to remain as it is and one thing be changed. Why then should we experience freedom? His answer is that, not having an infinite mind, we cannot see the way everything works together. We therefore cannot actually know all the factors that control our actions, and therefore are able to believe that we are free.

Comment

Does this sound familiar? Leibniz seems to have taken the 'Duhem–Quine approach' (see page 77) 200 years before either Duhem or Quine!

In his *Critique of Pure Reason*, Kant distinguished between:

- phenomena (things as we experience them), and
- noumena (things as they are in themselves).

He argued that the mind understands phenomena by means of the concepts (space, time and causality) that it imposes on experience. Thus we can say that everything has a cause, not because we have been able to check absolutely everything, but because our minds are so organized that they impose the idea of causality – that is the only way our minds can understand the world.

With Kant, choices are determined by our desires, beliefs and motives. Once made, they have inevitable consequences. Thus from the standpoint of the choosing subject, there is freedom, but from the standpoint of the observer (both in terms of observation of motives and in seeing the way in which actions dovetail into chains of causes) everything fits into a pattern in the phenomenal world, a pattern that automatically makes us look for causal determination.

Comment

Notice that both Leibniz and Kant are writing against a background of a rational and scientific view of the world (as expressed classically in Newtonian physics). They struggle to account for the experience of freedom in such a world. For Kant, it is made possible only by making a fundamental distinction between things in themselves and things as we perceive them: the former free, the latter determined. For Leibniz, freedom is an illusion born of our ignorance of the totality of causes acting upon us. Whereas for Descartes and Kant, freedom is real, for Leibniz it is not – and that makes his view rather closer to a more radical view of **determinism** that developed through the 19th and 20th centuries.

By the 19th century, however, the usual meaning of determinism was such as to remove all freedom from the acting subject. Determinism was simply the belief that everything that happens is determined by a necessary chain of causes. In this way, it came to be held that the mind (whatever role that played in action) was itself determined, rather than simply being influenced.

Whereas with Kant there are two worlds, in one of which the self could be free, by the end of the 19th century, there is a single, determined world in which freedom is an illusion caused by failure to understand the determining factors.

Scientific determinism

In *The Riddle of the Universe* (1899), Ernst Haeckel argued that everything, including thought, was the product of material world and was absolutely controlled and determined by its laws. Freedom was an illusion; scientific materialism was the only valid interpretation of reality. This view reflected both the success of science by the end of the 19th century and also its limitations. By the end of the 20th century, most scientists were being far more cautious in their claims.

In looking at 20th-century science, we have already seen that many thing in physics (e.g. the behaviour of sub-atomic particles) or in biology (e.g. genetic mutations) seem to happen in a random way. Chance replaces strict predictability. By the same token, once a chance event has taken place, other things follow from it in a necessary fashion. A classic exposition of this dual shaping of reality was given by **Jacques Monod** in his book *Chance and Necessity* (1972). Monod claims that the whole edifice of evolution, which to some appears to be the product of design, can be accounted for entirely by the operation of physical laws on the many chances that are thrown up by genetic mutation.

My experience of freedom may thus be explained in terms of chance (the particular circumstances in which I experienced myself as making a free choice) and necessity (the factors that, with hindsight, I can see as determining my choice).

The uncertainty principle

Heisenberg's uncertainty principle – that it is possible to know either the position or the momentum of a particle, but not to know both accurately at the same time – is often cited as an example of freedom at the very heart of modern quantum physics and, therefore, that determinism is generally inadequate. It is unwise to take press this argument, however. In part (as we saw earlier, page 84) there is a difference of interpretation, reflected in the debate between Einstein and Bohr in the 1930s, about whether such uncertainty reflects reality itself or only our ability to know reality. We also know that nature can be regular and predictable on the larger scale, even if at the sub-atomic level individual particles are undetermined.

Probability

We saw, in looking at the classic formulation of the problem of induction (e.g. in Hume), that there can be no such thing as absolute certainty, but only increasingly high degrees of probability. To formulate a general theory from observations requires a leap beyond the evidence itself, based on the assumption that the universe is predictable and uniform and that the more evidence is gathered for something, the more likely it will be that further evidence will confirm it. But no finite number of instances can logically require one to conclude an absolute law.

Apart from Monod, all the thinkers mentioned so far in this chapter lived prior to the end of the 19th century. Issues of freedom and determinism – particularly as they have come to be studied in ethics and the philosophy of religion – still rely significantly on arguments from that period. However, during the 19th century there were significant changes – particularly in the gathering and analysis of information about populations – that led to a very different approach to law and determinism, an approach that allowed indeterminism and probability to operate at an individual level, while claiming overall statistical theories to apply to large numbers. This not only influenced thinking in the social sciences, but had important implications for the emergence of modern physics, in particular quantum theory.

Particularly during the 19th century, there was a considerable increase in the recording of statistics about human life and death. Using these it became possible to formulate laws about human behaviour, in the same way as experimental evidence had provided the basis for physical laws. As we shall see later, this led to the establishment of the social sciences, as humankind became increasingly the object of scientific examination.

Ian Hacking, in *The Taming of Chance* (CUP, 1990), has shown this increasing use of statistical data and the way in which what, on an individual level, appeared to be a simple matter of random chance, became a piece of data to be interpreted as part of an overall statistical law. This had profound implications for an understanding of determinism, for we now have laws that are based not on an analysis of individual events, but on statistics which summarize large numbers of events. And, of course, statistics cannot be used to prove what happened in an individual situation, only to show its statistical probability.

EXAMPLE

In a general election, after the first few results are in (or even after a detailed 'exit poll' has been taken) commentators are predicting the result that can be expected. In seat after seat, patterns are watched and tabulated. It is deemed likely that the people voting in any one polling station will behave just like others up and down the country. However, for each individual entering the booth, there is an absolutely free choice.

How then can such freedom be reconciled with the statistical laws?

The sociologist Durkheim said of this phenomenon:

> Collective tendencies have an existence of their own; they are forces as real as cosmic forces.
>
> (*Suicide*, 1897)

Clearly, this has implications for looking at the human sciences, but notice the broader implication – that scientific laws can operate in terms of statistical averages, rather than on the ability to predict what will happen on each and every occasion.

Statistical information gives an accurate picture of the actions of a society, but it cannot show the actions of an individual within that society. In other words, laws can operate at different levels. What appears to be predictability, even determinism, at one level, can nevertheless coexist with indeterminism and unpredictability at another.

Key point

The results of statistical analysis show law-like tendencies, while allowing indeterminism at the level of the individual phenomenon being studied. In arguing for a general theory, it is not necessary to claim that it determines what happens on every occasion, only that it determines the probability that something will happen.

Science can deal in probabilities as well as certainties. This might have seemed curious to Newton, but it becomes inevitable in physics from the 20th century. What is more, the element of probability built into statistical evidence is in line with the process of inductive inference by which theories are produced (see Chapter 2).

Probability is also relevant to the way in which theories are modified or discarded. We saw earlier that there has been considerable debate about the validity of theories in the face of individual instances of conflicting evidence. This was one of the issues that divided Popper and Kuhn or Lakatos.

Once we are dealing with probability, it is not necessary that every piece of data should conform to a theory, just that – taken statistically – the theory should reflect what happens when a quantity of data is assessed.

Names

Your name is most improbable. Whatever you are called, there are a very large number of names that you were not given – so the chance of you having your name is very small indeed.

Contrariwise, given the wishes of your parents and perhaps other relatives, any established family traditions about naming, the traditions of your culture or religion and many other factors, the probability increases. Indeed, the very fact that you were born either male or female cut by almost half the number of choices open to your parents!

When every factor is weighed, including those coincidences for which no explanation can be given, your naming might be quite inevitable.

The more I know of your family and their reasons for giving the names they do, the more likely does your particular name become; the less I know, the less likely does your name become. A stranger's name may have been chosen randomly, for all I know.

Much the same thing applies to physical phenomena. On the one hand, they seem unlikely; on the other, under scientific investigation, they become inevitable.

For Durkheim, the 'laws' that could be known statistically were rather like a force of a certain strength, sufficient to produce a result in a limited number of cases, but not overwhelming of the individual. Some respond to that force, others do not – but statistically the number responding is predictable.

In effect, this approach amounts to a theory of influence. Statistical laws are in fact descriptions of degrees of influence that apply to individuals within their field. The degree to which this influence is effective will depend on many other factors. Thus the individual is not determined or predictable, while the overall trend is quantifiable.

EXAMPLE

Modern political and social theory gives many examples of this sort of argument. Young people from deprived backgrounds may be deemed more likely to commit acts of vandalism. That does not explain the individual choice to commit such acts, it simply suggests that deprived backgrounds tend to exert an influence in that direction.

Equally improbable!

If you claim that a law – for example, one of Newton's laws of motion – has universal application, then it must apply to an infinite number of situations. Every time you test one of these, the law is confirmed and therefore becomes a little more probable. By the same token, if it can apply to an infinite number of such situations, there will always be an infinite number that have not been tested (for infinity, less a finite number, is still infinity). Therefore you might argue that all universal theories are equally improbable!

Such a dilemma makes it important to find a method of assessing the probability of something being the case, given the evidence to hand – to which we now turn.

Calculating probability

Thomas Bayes (1702–1761) argued that the probability of something happening could be expressed mathematically, and that such probability equations are needed in order for inductive reasoning to work. 'Baysianism', the general theory of probability that became influential in the philosophy of science in the 20th century, is based on his work.

Basically, a rational person believes X to be the case to the degree that he or she believes 'not X' not to be the case – and thus the sum of the probability of these two opposites always equals 1. In a sense, this is obvious. But Baysian approaches take it a further step and assess what evidence it takes to change that belief. In effect, a single piece of evidence 'Y' should not automatically refute all belief in X. Rather the belief that X is the case should have a probability proportionate to the acceptance of both X and Y. In other words, you do not simply scrap and rethink all your beliefs with every new piece of evidence produced, but moderate them on a scale, taking that new evidence into account.

In other words

If I have a theory 'X' that predicts 'Y will happen', the degree to which the evidence for 'Y' confirms the theory 'X' will depend on the likelihood that Y would happen anyway, even if theory 'X' were wrong.

If the latter is the case, the theory 'X' is not well confirmed by that evidence, even if it predicted it. But, if 'Y' is extremely unlikely to happen unless 'X' is correct, then it offers very strong confirmation.

To put it crudely: it is no use expecting your new theory to be confirmed on the basis of its prediction that the Sun will rise tomorrow! If it is going to happen anyway, it cannot significantly increase the probability of your theory being correct.

EXAMPLE

Let us return to the familiar example of Eddington's eclipse observations which confirmed Einstein's theory that light coming from distant stars would be bent by the gravitational pull of the Sun. Without Einstein's theory, the probability of the light from the stars being bent in this way was very low indeed, since light had always been believed to travel in straight lines. Therefore the observation that this was in fact the case provided the strongest possible confirmation that Einstein's theory was correct.

The most popular version of Baysianism is the **subjective** Baysian approach. This argues that the probability calculations refer to the degrees of belief that scientists have in a particular theory. In other words, it provides a way of ascertaining whether it is reasonable to believe a theory to be true.

Chaos and complexity

Ideas of a world in which everything happens by chance and is in a state of constant flux are not new. Among the ancients, Epicurus held this view. The whole Epicurean approach to life and ethics was based on the assumption that the world did not display a fixed regularity or purpose (as the Stoics claimed), but was a matter of chance.

We also saw earlier how, particularly at the sub-atomic level, the behaviour of individual particles was not predictable (or even measurable), even if sufficiently large numbers could yield statistical probability.

When we move on to consider chaos theory, the situation is in some ways reversed. When considering probability, you consider the patterning of large numbers and draw out statistical conclusions. By contrast, chaos theory looks at the large-scale implications of small-scale changes.

Chaos theory explores the way in which a minute change can bring about radically different effects, making prediction impossible. It was given popular exposure through the work of Edward Lorenz in the 1960s, who examined the effects of turbulence in dynamic systems, such as weather forecasting. He described chaos as a 'sensitive dependence' on initial conditions and produced the most popular image of this: the flapping of a butterfly's wing in Brazil causing a tornado in Texas. Chaos results from a system of regular feedback, which magnifies the initial variation again and again.

A mundane example of dependence on initial conditions would be ten pin bowling. However skilled you may be at bowling, there will always be minute changes in the angle at which you release the ball, that will be magnified as the ball travels the length of the lane. As it strikes, the first skittle falls back either slightly to the right of the left and the ball is deflected slightly in the other direction. From then on, within a fraction of a second, skittles start falling in different direction, sometimes hitting others as they fall.

The differences in the final arrangement of skittles each time is difficult to predict from the slight variation of angle as the ball leaves the bowler's hand. Even those who can achieve strike after strike, actually achieve a different strike every time, for the skittles will never fall in exactly the same way twice.

In a truly sensitive system, the amount of variation goes far beyond that of the crude bowling analogy. Every tiny change is magnified again and again in a way that yields a completely unpredictable result. Even though each of those changes is mathematically simple, prediction becomes impossible. Hence: chaos.

However, small changes can sometimes work together in quite a different way. Complexity theory is particularly associated with Ilya Prigogine (*Exploring Complexity*, W.H. Freeman, 1989) and it has implications for our understanding of many areas, for example evolution.

Complexity theory is the study of structure, order and stability. The world is actually full of such structures, although they are composed of smaller components which (certainly if you go down to the sub-atomic level) are far from predictable. Why is this?

In complexity theory, small changes gradually accumulate in such a way that a pattern emerges across a large number of individual changes. It can now be shown, for example by computer simulations, how elaborate life forms can assemble themselves by the operation of simple choices. This would go to explain how nature can have the appearance of design, even when there appears to be no designer. The complex patterning which we see as design is the product of a large number of simple operations.

Complexity and disorder

According to the Second Law of Thermodynamics, there is a gradual increase in randomness and disorder: everything is gradually expending energy and running down. How then can complexity increase?

It is argued that this cannot happen in a closed system, but only in open and adaptive systems. These are systems that are open to their environment and take in energy. If a human being is sealed against its environment, it will quickly cease to live and the body will gradually disorganize or decompose. Its complexity is maintained because it is constantly relating to what is around it. Therefore, although there may be a gradual winding down universally, with increasing disorder and entropy, there can be pockets of increasing complexity.

EXAMPLE

DNA is a fine example of a self-organizing system. It has the ability to reproduce itself and create more and more complex organisms – indeed, the complexity of genetic information relates directly to the complexity of the organism it is able to create (along with a great deal of information that, as far as we are aware, has no direct part to play in determining features of the organism). So DNA is able to work against the Second Law of Thermodynamics – creating greater complexity, by sending out instructions which determine how available material may be organized into a living being.

DNA does not construct a body; DNA simply gives the instructions that enable a body to construct itself – complexity at work.

The principles that determine the operation of a complex entity only emerge at that degree of complexity, not at a lower level. In other words, you will never discover anything about human behaviour from the analysis of a small piece of human tissue. A study of complexity is the very opposite of a reductionist approach. A complex entity works at the level of its maximum not its minimum complexity. If you want to know about patterns of congestion on a highway, don't start by analysing the internal combustion engine. Look at the way cars are used.

A significant issue here is whether one needs to step outside the process of complexity and design and look for an external designing force. Thus, for example, traditional Christian theology has seen the design as being given by God. Paul Davies and others have argued that complexity theory gives confirmation of a cosmic design. Wherever we look we see patterns and apparent design. This may no longer act as proof of some external designer, but it does suggest that there is an internal process of design which works itself out and is seen in the large scale, even where small-scale variations suggest that chance rules.

Comment

With complexity, however, design can be self-generated. Thus, for example, Richard Dawkins in *The Blind Watchmaker* (1986) and *Climbing Mount Improbable* (1996) has shown the development of complex forms, but without the need for any external designing agent. The natural feature of life to self-organize, and the inevitability of the rise of more and more complex forms over a period of time, is linked directly with the genetic basis of life. Our uniqueness and our 'design' is given through the very complex genetic code that determines how every cell in our body is to develop.

7 THE PHILOSOPHY OF BIOLOGY

An important starting point for any philosophy of biology is the examination of Darwin's theory of natural selection. It forms the basis of the more general modern understanding of the development of species, which combines Darwin's insights with the mechanism for variations, now understood in terms of genetic mutations. Genetics has also provided information about the development of complex biological organisms and their various characteristics, and about the relationship between one species and another.

In considering these issues, we may also need to be aware that it is within the biological sciences that many of the ethical dilemmas concerning science and technology have arisen. In particular, the ability of genetics to offer a way to modify living forms, with enormous implications for the control that humankind has over the environment as well as over its own health and the development of the human species, has raised the most profound questions about the nature of science and the criteria by which technologies should be evaluated.

Natural selection

In terms of its origins, Darwin's theory of natural selection seems (as many brilliant new insights do with the benefit of hindsight) to be quite straightforward. He started his argument by observing the amazing variety of, for example, dogs or flowers, that humans were able to bring about through selective breeding. He then sought to discover how the same process might account for the wide variety of living forms in nature. What he needed to find was a mechanism within nature as a whole, which corresponded to the selective breeding carried out in the domestic sphere by the gardener or farmer.

The process of struggle for existence (as it had been outlined by Malthus) in the face of limited resources led to his perception that in any struggle certain favoured individuals are able to survive and breed, at the expense of those not so favoured. He saw also that the key feature of success was the ability of a species to adapt to its environment. Those variations in individual members of a species which favoured them in competing for limited resources were likely to lead to survival into adulthood, the chances of successful breeding and, therefore, of the wider dissemination of those particular variations in the population as a whole. Thus, the process of selective breeding by humans was being carried out by large, impersonal forces within the natural order as a whole.

Problems with natural selection

Initially, Darwin's theory met opposition not primarily on the grounds that there was anything wrong with his argument, but in light of the more fundamental question of whether any theory for the development of species was necessary at all. Largely on religious grounds, but also as a common-sense response to the observation of the amazing variety of living forms, it was assumed that each species had been created distinct from the others. Much of science had been involved with the listing and classification of species. Rather than developing in such a way as to adapt to their environment, it was assumed that each species was designed in order to make its continued existence possible.

To a large extent, arguments about purpose within the natural world had been in retreat since the rise of modern science. We saw earlier how the mechanical view of the universe, epitomized in Newtonian physics, had replaced the sense of order and purpose, in which everything had a 'final cause', that was the mediaeval legacy of Aristotelianism.

Even if such purpose had been eliminated from the operation of physical laws, it remained in terms of the design of living things. Now, with Darwin's argument, a mechanism had been found which appeared make all reference to external design irrelevant. The mechanical and mathematical approach, which had swept aside the older mediaeval view of a world full of purpose, now seemed to engulf all living things, humankind included. That required a major rethinking of previous philosophy. Initial opposition to Darwin was therefore not limited to those of a conservative religious disposition.

The other problem with Darwin's theory was the lack of fossil evidence for transitional states between species. Hence, judging by the majority of fossils found, it would be more realistic to see species as appearing in a distinct form, rather than seeing them as the result of a long period of gradual change.

Of course, there is a natural explanation for this lack of evidence. Before humans developed burial rituals and the embalming of corpses, most species simply died and were left to rot or were eaten by other species. Left to its own devices a body is soon reduced to bones and those bones eventually become dust, so that no trace remains. It is only in the rare circumstances of a body being preserved (e.g. by being trapped in a bog) that we find a fossil.

One might also argue that evolution did not take place incrementally, but in short bursts, interspersed with longer periods of relative stability. Thus, given that the transition between species is faster than the persistence of that species once more or less formed and given that, of the millions and millions of specimens that live, only a handful are going to end up as fossils, it is only realistic that we should find few, if any, transitional state fossils.

Darwin's theory is presented in a logical way and in effect invites the reader to go along with it and then to examine the balance of probability that it is correct. Natural selection was never a theory born out of the interpretation of a vast array of fossil evidence, but rather, it emerged out of observation and analogy which, once tested out against subsequent evidence, gradually took on the force of an absolute conviction.

Comment

In *The Beak of the Finch* (Cape, 1994), Jonathan Weiner describes a 20-year study of finches on one of the Galapagos Islands, the place where Darwin first gathered the information that led to his theory of natural selection. Weiner gave detailed information about the small differences in the length of beaks, showing, for example, that in times of drought only those finches with the longest beaks could succeed in getting the toughest seeds and therefore survived to breed. What is amazing is that only a very small difference (less than a millimetre in length) in beak size can make the difference between life and death in times of severe competition for limited food. Bringing this sort of research up to date, DNA samples taken from the blood of various finches showed the genetic differences that corresponded to their physical abilities and characteristics of each type of finch. Here we have a modern piece of research which provides additional data to illustrate Darwin's original observation.

But those data come to hand simply because the modern scientist already knows what to observe and record. It is a good example of using a theory in order to select relevant data. That is not, in itself, an illogical thing to do – indeed, it is the only thing one can do.

Quite apart from detailed studies such as Weiner's, there are many examples today of the process of natural selection. Whereas the evolution of different species happens over long periods and is therefore not open to straightforward observation, there are some forms of life that mutate and establish themselves very quickly, for example in the case of new strains of existing diseases. Every now and then a new strain of 'flu' emerges and it is able to flourish because it is sufficiently different from the previous one to render existing immunization programmes ineffective. Faced with a hostile (well-immunized) environment, only those varieties of a virus that are not affected by immunization will survive and develop.

A tautology?

There is a common misunderstanding of Darwin's theory of natural selection, related particularly to the phrase 'survival of the fittest' (a phrase which, incidentally, was coined by Herbert Spencer rather than Darwin). This takes the form of the criticism that 'survival of the fittest' is a tautology; in other words, that the phrase is a proposition defining what one means by fitness.

Now if this were true, it would be a significant criticism, but it is based on a misunderstanding. The expression 'survival of the fittest' can indeed describe Darwin's theory, but it is not a proposition (if it were, it would indeed be a tautology). In other words, his is not a theory that argues that, in some way, the fittest 'should' survive, neither does it somehow ascribe a quality 'fitness' to those who survive. The phrase 'survival of the fittest' is simply a description of what is observed.

In other words, within a population that includes characteristics that vary, those variations that happen to enable an individual to survive to adulthood will enhance the chances that the individual will breed, and will therefore increase the incidence of those variations in the next generation. 'Survival of the fittest' is therefore simply the summary of an observed process.

Causes and purposes

One of the interesting offshoots of discussion of natural selection is a comparison of the evolutionary and purposive aspects of biological phenomena. As we saw earlier, one of the features of natural selection is that it provides an impersonal mechanism for producing the appearance of design. But how does that affect how we describe those features of species which appear to have a purpose?

Some animals, for example, have colouring which helps them to blend into their surroundings, thus enabling them to hide from predators. In common speech, one might say that the 'purpose' of that colour is for defence. Similarly, I need to keep my body temperature within certain limits. If I get too hot, I go red, the pores of my skin are dilated and I sweat, thus releasing heat. I also get thirsty – a sign that my body needs to take in water in order to replace the fluids that are being lost.

One could go on to describe many features of the body in terms of what they are 'there to do'. In other words, that everything – from the hair on your head, to the way your toes are jointed – is there for a purpose related to your well-being. From this perspective, each feature of a living thing has a purpose, which is its contribution to the overall aim of maintaining the life of the individual animal or plant.

The impact of natural selection on such features is to suggest that they have a cause rather than a purpose, natural selection having favoured those individuals which displayed advantageous features. In other words, I have certain qualities and bits of me perform certain functions in order to promote my well-being, simply because – through natural selection – they have been qualities and functions that have promoted survival and have therefore survived and spread within the gene stock of my species.

EXAMPLE

In the green of the jungle, vulnerable animals that are brightly coloured are quickly seen and eaten. Those that are green, tend to get overlooked, grow to adulthood and breed. Hence the colour whose 'purpose' appears now as camouflage, is selected naturally.

The genetic basis of life

In Chapter 1, we looked briefly at the impact of genetics on the biological sciences. In terms of the philosophy of biology, it has provided an explanation for the random variations that enable natural selection (thereby acting as confirmation for that theory) and also shows the fundamental interconnectedness of all living things.

Deoxyribonucleic acid (DNA)

All living things are composed of chemical substances, of which the nucleic acids (RNA and DNA) and proteins determine the way in which living cells are put together. In the nucleus of each cell (except for sperm, egg and red blood cells) are 23 pairs of chromosomes which contain the DNA, made up of two strands of chemical units called nucleotides, spiralled into a double helix. The 'information' given by the DNA takes the form of sequences of nucleotides (genes).

Human DNA comprises about 30,000 active genes, which give the code for making 20 different amino acids, which themselves produce the proteins, making us what we are. But these are only a small part of the total information contained in DNA. Between 95% and 97% of the nucleotide sequence is regarded as 'junk DNA' and is not used in the construction of a human being. Most has been left behind in the evolutionary process, giving theoretical instructions that are no longer needed and are therefore deleted.

The strands of DNA are around six feet in length and the genetic information is given by sequences of the four chemicals (bases), adenine, thymine, guanine and cytosine. The whole human genome is thus a digital code made from those sequences of chemicals – a total sequence of around 3.5 billion pieces of information!

Confirming Darwin

The theory of natural selection showed how, given a number of variations within individuals in a species, those with particular advantages would survive and breed. What Darwin did not know was the reason for the small physical changes that had such a profound effect on the fate of individuals and through them on evolutionary progress as a whole. Now, with genetic theory, we see the way in which random mutations occur.

As cells reproduce, the chromosomes work in pairs to copy the information required. Generally, where one of them produces a defective copy, the other provides a good one. From time to time, however, a defective copy survives and (in response to defective instructions) one of the amino acids in a protein chain is changed for another. This is termed a mutation. Mostly these lead to irregular growths in tissues, but if a mutation takes place in a germ cell (which is rare) then that change can be inherited.

Most mutations either make no difference or are neutral, as far as the individual possessing them is concerned. Just once in a while they make a positive difference, work well alongside the rest of the genes in the 'gene pool' of that particular species, improve survival chances and thus shape up the future generations of a species.

Thus genetics has provided a crucial underpinning for natural selection.

The interconnectedness of life

One of the most interesting results of the publishing of the complete human genome is the recognition of just how many genes we share with other creatures, even very simple ones, and the way in which the same gene that is used to store memories for a fruit fly, for example, is also used to store memories in a human being.

There is one obvious but significant conclusion to draw from this, namely that it reinforces the general view of evolutionists that all forms of life are closely linked. Thus the identical functioning gene in two very different species must have been developed before those two species separated off. In other words, there was a common ancestor of both which had that gene for that function and passed it on to two very different future species.

It is no longer necessary to examine the fossil record or agree with the debate about whether there is sufficient evidence to show that Darwin's theory of natural selection is correct. The fact of evolution is there to be seen plainly in the nature and functioning of our genes, for genes have a history that goes back far beyond the start of this one particular species.

Getting closer

If we wanted proof that all species are linked, we can look at the shared DNA between creatures. Chimpanzees have DNA which is 98.9% identical to that of humans.

This also means that we have a new route by which to trace the development and splitting off of species from one another. The degree to which two species share common genetic information is a good indicator of how long ago they diverged from one another. We have more in common with other species than that which makes us different.

In terms of the philosophy of science, the main contribution here is the confirmation of the Darwinian theory of evolution by natural selection. By the same token, the overall view of humankind and its place within the world is profoundly changed by the recognition of its shared genetic heritage. Perhaps this has implications that are more appropriately explored in terms of the philosophy of religion or ethics.

The human genome

One of the major events of the end of the 20th century was the analysis of the human genome, a public draft of which was finally published in June 2000. The intention behind this project was as much practical as based on 'pure' science – namely, that a knowledge of the operation of each of the human genes could lead to the prevention of inherited diseases, such as cystic fibrosis.

It is difficult to imagine any single scientific discovery equal to the setting down of the human genome. The genome is no more or less than the full set of information required to create a living human being. That life can be the product of a sequence of bits of information is remarkable in itself – and one must then ask what this does for self-understanding. Uniqueness (we are all different) and interconnectedness (all living things share common DNA) are just the two extremes of the scale of ways in which this can be understood and appreciated.

Basically, genetic information determines the form and operation of living things – and thus must play a significant part in their medical history. It may be able to indicate a predisposition to certain forms of illness and also predict genetic abnormalities in the unborn. It therefore offers a degree of control over the human body that is more fundamental and subtle than the traditional invasive operation of medicine. In a sense, genetics might lead the body to be taught how to heal itself, rather than attempt to force that healing through surgical removal of disease, or treatment with drugs.

It also brings the process of the application of science very close to the sense of identity of each individual. Forensic examination uses the fact that genetic information is unique to each individual and can therefore act as a means of identification from sample tissues.

Some implications of genetics

One of the key questions related to genetics is the degree to which we are the product of genetic information, as opposed to environment or training. This, of course, has social and political implications, especially for those who take a basically socialist (or Marxist) view that human life is largely determined by material and social conditions and therefore that people can change themselves by changing their circumstances. The fear expressed from this point of view (see page 132, on sociobiology) is that the more human behaviour is conditioned by genetic factors, the less one can be held responsible for it. This, of course, is yet another form of the freedom versus determinism debate (see page 107).

One of the great turning points in the scope of philosophical enquiry came in the 1970s, when there was a progressive recognition that philosophy needed to address a number of social and political areas of life, rather than (as had been the case for the decades before that) being focused more narrowly on the meaning and use of terms. In other words, philosophy was expected to have something to say about human situations, not merely about the language other people used when commenting on those situations. This movement was given particular impetus in the fields of medical and nursing ethics – and these are, naturally enough, still the areas in which the implications of genetic research are felt most acutely.

Part of the anxiety expressed about treatment at the genetic level has to do with the pace at which the knowledge is being gained and applied and perhaps the fear of a 'Frankenstein' approach to humanity, where science seeks to construct life artificially. Already, of course, there is great scope for that to take place, in the area of *in vitro* fertilization, for example, where conception becomes possible in circumstances where a couple would formerly have remained childless. It also raises issues such as the right of those who have passed child-bearing age to have fertilized eggs implanted so that they may bear children.

Key points

- Do I control my genes or am I controlled by them?
- What are the implications of the predictability of future health? Should genetic information be provided to insurance companies or be required as a condition of employment?
- What are the implications of a genetic revolution in the diagnosis and treatment of illness?
- What implications, if any, does genetics have for the sense of human freedom?

Sociobiology

Sociobiology, the title of a book published in 1975, is the exploration of biological and evolutionary factors in the development of society. Its author, Edward Wilson, analysed social behaviour from ants to humans. Had he limited his work to animal behaviour, he would have avoided criticism, but his last 30 pages were devoted to looking at how his theory could be applied to human society. It therefore became a hugely controversial book, because it implied that people were not all born the same, but were biologically suited for particular roles. If differences in people's social position could be attributed to biological programming, the ideals of democracy and racial and sexual equality seemed to be threatened. Apart from the controversy, however, it was an immensely important work, because it systematically examined social behaviour as a biological phenomenon.

Note

In effect, Wilson was exploring the chemical 'language' by which, for example, different ants within a colony knew what they should do. Their roles were not learned, they were quite instinctive and could be triggered by giving them an appropriate chemical stimulus.

The application of evolutionary principles to human society was not new, having been explored by Herbert Spencer in the 19th century. From a viewpoint informed by modern molecular biology, however, it can be argued that, whatever we feel we should do – even if it appears to be from completely moral and altruistic motives – is in fact a prompting of our genes, and is related to the need for survival.

A exposition of the key issues here is found in Richard Dawkins' *The Selfish Gene*. According to Dawkins, our genes are inherently 'selfish', in that their task is to promote survival and successful reproduction. Our bodies are, from a genetic point of view, vehicles that aid the survival and development of our genetic material. It is certainly not right to see 'selfish' as a moral term here (although it has sometimes been interpreted that way). Dawkins is not saying that genetic theory somehow causes and therefore justifies 'selfish' behaviour on the part of human individuals.

There is, however, within sociobiology, a recognition that genes are promoted through the success in breeding of the individuals that carry them. The most obvious example of us acting in line with our genetic programming is in the sphere of sexuality. Males are likely to feel the urge to seek out as many sexual partners as possible, since their supply of sperm is constantly renewed and the most sensible way of making sure of a good number of progeny is to share it as widely as possible. Although prudence may suggest that it is not ideal to conceive a child with every sexually attractive female within grabbing distance, the fundamental urge to do so is still present.

By contrast, females can only produce a limited number of children. Hence it might be important for them to secure the help of a male who will not only impregnate her, but also provide some measure of protection for her offspring. Traditionally, therefore, males have gone for quantity and females for quality!

One could also examine the sexual taboo against incest on the same basis. If a sexual union is unlikely to produce a child that is genetically viable, then it is biologically discouraged and this finds its expression in social and religious rules.

Morality steps in and tries to regulate the sexual jungle – but is that not just another attempt to maximize the number of successfully reared offspring? One might argue that, in terms of the survival of society as a whole, some restraint may actually promote the welfare of the next generation.

Note

Remember the distinction between purpose and cause in the philosophy of biology. The 'purpose' of sexual attraction is the conception of children and thus the continuation of the genetic stock. But, following the general way of arguing about the qualities of living things, this may be simply be 'caused' by a process of natural selection. In other words, those with no sexual attractiveness or drive are less likely to breed.

There is also a danger that issues within sociobiology will fall into the same trap as the 'tautology' criticism of the 'survival of the fittest' (see page 125). The sociobiological approach is not saying that certain genes 'ought' to survive or that 'survival' is what genes are for, simply that – as a matter of observation – those genetic traits that promote the survival and breeding of individuals in a competitive environment will themselves survive.

It may be argued that a distinctive feature of human society is the capacity of individuals to show altruism and co-operation rather than rivalry. The response to this is straightforward. If helping others, or even giving up one's own life for the sake of others, is what one feels impelled to do, that too may be seen as promoting the overall benefit of the genetic pool, since a society where everyone was 'selfish' in the narrow sense might well be self-destructive.

EXAMPLE

Take the case of a mother who loses her life in the attempt to save her child from drowning. At one level, that appears to be an absolutely unselfish act. But it could be argued that we are genetically programmed to sacrifice ourselves for the sake of the continuation of our genes. Such an act is no more than a cell is required to do when it grows in the wrong place or is no longer needed. Individuals are expendable, it is the ongoing genetic stream that counts.

Perhaps that example is too obvious, because the child to be saved (whether the rescue is successful or not) is a direct genetic descendant. What is the person drowning is a stranger? Here, one might argue that – within the human species – it is sometimes necessary for individuals to sacrifice themselves for the sake of the whole. Even if it is not their genes directly, it is at least the genetic make-up of the species that is being protected.

Genes are there to preserve and protect their own kind. Our emotional and moral promptings are merely the way in which we experience and respond to those genetic promptings. We may feel that we are being rational, independent of our basic biological urges, but sociobiology would challenge that.

(Why anyone would throw away their life in order to save an animal is, of course, another matter.)

The genetic environment

An additional problem with the application of technologies based on genetics concerns the social and environmental factors that need to be taken into account. A good example of this is the debate over genetically modified food crops. Artificially engineered genetic modifications result in species with characteristics that would not have developed naturally. For example, genetic modification can involve the use of genes from very different species that would never normally have been able to cross-fertilize. That is all very well, but it is possible that the resulting species could cross-fertilize with others, with quite unknowable consequences. The issue here is that of interconnectedness. Genetics has shown the fundamental sameness of all living things, but genetic research generally seeks to produce a life form that is immune from unwanted influence from its environment. To create a plant that is unaffected by disease may do wonders for one's production of crops, but it is to create a species that is out of step with the surrounding process of genetic change.

EXAMPLE

In 1997, a Canadian farmer reported that seeds from genetically modified oil-seed rape had cross-pollinated with weeds that were growing nearby. This was tested and found to be the case. Although an isolated incident, it has enormous implications. The resulting weed would have benefited from the genes that were designed to make the rape plants resistant to herbicides (thus allowing the crops to be sprayed to kill off weeds, without being affected themselves). In other words a kind of 'superweed' that would be able to resist herbicides would have been produced.

One way to avoid such problems is to create sterile crops that are incapable of producing seed once they have grown to maturity. This preserves the environment, but produces another interesting moral dilemma – for such crops depend upon a supply of new seed each year, but seeds cannot be taken from them and used for planting the next crop. This, in effect, makes the crop 'copyright', sold in order to produce a single yield. This would have great benefit for those who supply seed, but would harm those (particularly in poorer countries) who depend on the ongoing harvesting of seed rather than paying for new seed for each planting.

The philosophy of biology is clearly one of the most challenging areas of study, not least because of the rate at which technological developments and moral issues are generated by molecular biology. Whereas in the 1950s, 1960s and 1970s the contribution of science and technology was particularly controversial in the area of physics, with the ever-escalating threat of nuclear weapons, in the 1990s and into the 21st century, the controversies have tended to shift far more in the direction of biology – both in terms of human self-understanding and, as we have seen, in the technologies concerned with the human body and the environment.

It is appropriate, therefore, to move on at this point to look more generally at the way in which science has come to look at humankind.

8 SCIENCE AND HUMANKIND

Most of what we have been considering so far relates to how human beings understand the world around them. Yet this has always presupposed certain things about humankind: it is concerned with what is 'out there' to be known, but also with the process (through the action of the senses and the mind) by which we come to know it. Thus Descartes' dualism of mind and body or Kant's idea of the mind imposing categories on experience, or Aristotle's view of 'final causes' explore the ways in which human minds make sense of the world. So any understanding of science implies an epistemology (theory of knowledge) and also a philosophy of mind.

From the time of **Galen** (129–210 CE), who combined the work of a doctor with that of a philosopher, the human body and mind have been the object of scientific study. In this chapter, therefore, we shall outline some of the issues that arise when human beings use science to try to understand themselves.

Prior to the 19th century the discussion was of the nature and operation of the physical body and of the relationship between mind and body – as well as the more general philosophical issues of human behaviour, in ethics and politics. But since the 19th century the range of scientific approaches has expanded, to include psychology and sociology and – with the impact of evolution – on the nature of human origins and the relationship between humankind and other species.

Alongside this (although beyond the scope of the present book) we need to keep in mind that science and technology have taken an increasingly active role in shaping human well-being and experience. Information technology, for example, has transformed social communications.

Comment

The relationship between science and humankind involves two related processes, both of which are circular and work rather like a 'feedback' loop that can be set up if the microphone of an audio system is positioned too near a speaker:

- Scientific knowledge is shaped by the way the human mind works. To understand itself in a scientific way, therefore, the mind has to turn its own cognitive powers in upon itself. This creates all sorts of problems – for example, in the claim that a reductionist analysis (which might claim that thoughts and choices are no more than the firing of certain neurones in the brain) is inadequate to account for the complexity of and the experience of what it is to be human. This is really saying that one aspect of the way we understand things (by analysis) is inadequate to account for the whole of the way we are.
- Science examines a phenomenon (human life) which is shaped by science. A social scientist may analyse a problem and the media communicate it in a way that actually influences the problem being examined. To take a sociological example, those who are told that they come from a deprived background may start to think of themselves in that particular way and react accordingly.

These loops in the process by which science examines humanity have parallels with the issues facing particle physics, where the act of investigation itself determines what is found.

The human machine

Although writing in the second century CE, Galen was quite capable of examining parts of the body and considering their function in terms of what they contributed to the whole. Sometimes, of course, he was wrong. For example, he assumed that the purpose of the heart was to create heat and that the lungs drew in cool air in order to stop the body overheating. But he had established an important feature with an examination of anything as complex as the human body – namely that it had to be considered as a whole, and that all the parts were there to serve some overall purpose.

His views on the heart were overturned when, following years of experimentation, William Harvey published *De Motu Cordis* in 1628, establishing that the heart was a pump, and that blood was oxygenated in the lungs before being pumped through the body. This enabled progress to be made in analysing the workings of the body, for it became clear that each organ was nourished by oxygenated blood and that the whole body was thus an interconnected system.

In one important respect Galen and Harvey were taking a similar approach, namely that each part of the body could be understood in terms of its function within the whole. But the difference between them is also significant. Galen observed and tried to understand the purpose of each organ. This was natural enough, since Aristotle had argued that each thing had its 'final cause' or purpose. What he did not show, however, was the mechanism that brought this about. In common with other features of the science of the 17th and 18th centuries, Harvey's work on the human body showed that it could be examined as a mechanism. Like the universe as a whole, the body was being seen as a machine. At the same time, Descartes was working on his philosophy that was to separate the unextended mind from the extended physical body, with the latter able to be examined like any other machine, controlled by mechanical laws.

Reductionist and holistic approaches

As we have already seen (page 93), in a reductionist analysis complex entities are reduced to their component parts. On this basis, I am nothing more than the sum total of all the cells of which my body is made. Now this approach fits perfectly well with seeing the body as essentially a machine. The living cells with which biology is concerned can be reduced to the chemical compounds of which they are made and then further reduced to the constituent atoms, which follow the laws of physics.

Thus, in this approach, although the human body is complex, its operations can ultimately be analysed in terms of the universal laws of physics.

An holistic approach, by way of contrast, examines the way in which complex entities operate. It looks at features that only appear at the level of the whole complex organism.

From the holistic point of view, a human being has a personal life that is quite different from those of the individual cells of which it is made up.

EXAMPLE

No amount of analysis of the effects of solar radiation on individual tissues or the protective qualities of melanin is going to explain why people choose to take a holiday and lie on a beach!

Sunburn can ruin that holiday; but your social life and the well-being of individual cells on the surface of your skin – although they can sometimes impinge on one another most intimately – are operating at very different levels. However it may feel at the time, there is more to you than sunburn!

Clearly, therefore, the two ways of considering human beings are not mutually exclusive. Whether it is mild sunburn or a serious cancer, the behaviour of individual cells is significant for the operation of the whole body. Equally, a holistic event (e.g. getting excited or worried about something) has an immediate effect on many of our bodily systems.

It does mean, however, that physical analysis is not the only scientific approach to understanding human beings. Hence we shall move progressively away from the level of bodies and DNA and towards the psychological, social, political and global aspects of human life.

Human origins and evolution

In terms of human self-understanding, Darwin's *Origin of Species* must rank as an absolutely pivotal work. A general understanding of evolution puts humankind in a global perspective, revealed in the stock of genetic code shared by all living things. Since the 19th century there has also been considerable development, through the discovery and analysis of early remains, of our own species over what is (in evolutionary terms) a very short period of time.

A chronological overview

The Earth was formed about five billion years ago; dry land and then primitive vegetation developed about 410 million years ago. So for most of its life, the planet has been watery and lifeless.

The progressive evolution of living things has been punctuated by major destructions at 250 million years ago (approximately 90 per cent of species destroyed) and 65 million years ago (most famous for bringing to an end the era of the dinosaurs, but destroying approximately 50 per cent of other species as well). Mammals only appeared 50 million years ago and the first apes 35 million years ago.

Somewhere between seven and four million years ago there lived in Africa (since that is where all remains older than about two million years have been found) a species of ape that was to see its descendants branch off into two different groups – the one to become modern chimpanzees and the other to become *Homo sapiens*. (Molecular clocks in DNA show that the human/chimpanzee differentiation took place less than 7 million years ago – before that we were a single species.)

Australopithecus (found in Ethiopia) dates from around 4 million years ago (with a brain capacity increase from 450, in the early apes, to around 750cc). One million years ago, *Homo erectus* is found in Africa, Asia and Europe (the brain capacity increasing from 800 to around 1200 cc), already shaping stones and using fire.

Neanderthal man probably developed up to 300,000 years ago (according to dating of Neanderthal remains in Spain) and by 75,000 years ago had burial places and funeral rites. That branch of the human family is generally thought to have become extinct about 32,000 years ago. What is not known at this stage is whether the earlier *Homo erectus* colonized Europe and developed into the Neanderthal branch there or whether that change happened elsewhere.

Homo sapiens appears in East and South Africa, about 100,000 years ago (or perhaps earlier) and by now his brain capacity has reached around 1400cc, much as it is today. It is assumed that he moved out from there to colonize the other continents.

The Australian branch

Australian examples of rock art may be up to 75,000 years old, although settlement in Australia was generally dated at about 50,000 years ago. A stone tool found there is thought to be up to 176,000 years old. If this is correct, it goes against any neat theory of migration. *Homo erectus* (rather than *Homo sapiens*) must have made his way to Australia. But that would have involved making some sort of craft to sail across at least 40 miles of ocean, which, in turn, would imply speech and social organization of some sort – features that were thought not to have developed until *Homo sapiens*.

This illustrates the fundamental problem with the scientific study of human origins – a very small quantity of physical remains is used as the basis for major theories of development and migration. One stone tool can cause chaos!

In general, there is some disagreement about whether modern man developed in Africa and then spread across the globe from there, or whether he developed from Neanderthal man in Europe and from *Homo erectus* in the Far East. Either way, we are dealing with very long periods of time, compared with which recorded history is only the most fleeting of moments.

By around 30,000 BCE we find cave paintings in south-west France (although, of course, if the Australian claims are correct, European culture was late developing) and by 10,000 BCE we find settled communities within the 'fertile crescent' of the Middle East. And the rest is history!

Methodology

Notice the scientific methodology used in examining human origins. First of all, we have archaeology and the problem here – as with the more general issue of the fossil record of evolutionary change – is that there is very little physical evidence on which to build theories.

As we saw earlier, in connection with the Australian finds, a small piece of conflicting evidence can seem to threaten an entire theory of human development and migration. Here we need to reflect on the issues examined in Chapter 3. A straightforward process of falsification might suggest that a single stone tool is enough to require that a theory be abandoned (on a simplified version of Popper's 'falsification' approach). Contrariwise, following Kuhn, one might wait for further evidence to make the overall paradigm no longer viable – in a sense, the contrary evidence is put 'on hold' until more is found.

Second, we need to keep in mind the potential problems involved with the human interpretation of humanity. We may bring our own understanding of what a tool is or what it takes to cross a stretch of water as a model for understanding the past – and thus read into the evidence more than we should.

Once finds of human origins are made and dated, there is analysis of, for example, the size and shape of a skull in order to find out brain capacity. Forensic examination of remains can yield information related to diet, body shape, posture and so on. A comparison of these then goes to build up developmental patterns – for example, the increase in brain capacity.

Such examination can build up a picture of the life of early humans. One danger in this process is the assumption of a neat and orderly development from one form to another. Thus, for example, it may be assumed that Neanderthal man was very unsophisticated compared with homo sapiens, who would have lived alongside him and eventually came to replace him in Europe. But this is an assumption influenced by evolutionary theory. It may eventually be seen that Neanderthal life was rather more sophisticated than we originally thought.

Evolution

From the start, it was clear that the theory of natural selection had important implications for human self-understanding and most of the early controversies were related to this. Darwin himself explored the implications of his theory for human development. In *The Descent of Man* (1871) and *The Expression of the Emotions* (1872) he suggested that mental ability and social behaviour could have the same form of evolutionary development over time as the physical body.

This application is often termed 'social Darwinism'. This approach was developed by **Herbert Spencer** (1820–1903). His own theory of evolution was based on Lamark's idea that one could inherit characteristics that had been developed by one's parents, which was to be superseded by Darwin's 'natural selection' theory. Nevertheless, his approach to social issues is one that has implications for any theory of evolution.

According to Spencer it was only natural that human society should follow the struggle for survival that went on throughout nature. In America he became hugely popular for his advocacy of free competition in a capitalist system; success and failure were part of the struggle to evolve. In social and economic terms, one should not feel guilty about succeeding at the expense of others, for this was the pattern throughout nature. To act in any other way was to stand in the way of progress. In Britain, he opposed the Poor Laws and state education, on the grounds that it gave benefit to those who were least able to take care of themselves and thus upset the natural competitive balance in society.

The general criticism of this approach is that it attempts to make what did in fact happen the logical basis for saying what ought to happen. This is an issue for ethics rather than the philosophy of science, but briefly (following arguments put forward by David Hume and, at the beginning of the 20th century, by G.E. Moore) it is held that you cannot logically derive an 'ought' from an 'is' and that a description, in itself, is no basis for a moral prescription – which is known in ethics as the 'naturalistic fallacy'.

The sociobiological approach

As we saw earlier (page 132) sociobiology makes the connection between such social trends and the principles that govern the 'lower' level of genetic survival – in other words, social trends are to be seen as the outworking of genetic tendencies, rather than as operating according to a separate set of laws applying only to the social level.

On the one hand, there sometimes appears to be a conflict between the social urge (e.g. to be philanthropic) and the biological (to be 'selfish' and maintain the survival of one's own progeny in the face of competition for limited resources). This is experienced at the level of morality, where a natural urge is required to be socially contained. On the other, if the sociobiological approach is correct, what appears to be 'higher' or more social forms of conditioning are merely the outworking in large populations of impulses that come from the basic urge of genes to survive.

This is one of the most interesting points at which science and morality come into close contact, with the temptation of moral philosophy to distance its concerns from the biological level and the biologist claiming that moral philosophy is, in a sense, simply a social phenomenon that reflects biological need.

A valuable mistake?

The temptation to commit a 'naturalist fallacy' is illustrated by considering the human implications of evolution as a whole. Professor Steve Jones sets out the modern case for evolution in his book *Almost Like a Whale* (Doubleday, 1999). To put it at its most basic, he describes life as 'a series of successful mistakes'. The various chances thrown up by genetic mutations gradually accumulate and those that are favourable give rise to others and so on. Gradually, evolution allows new species to emerge and we arrive at humankind.

The whole process leading up to humankind therefore depends on errors in copying sequences of chemicals on strands of DNA – the 'mistakes'. It may be tempting to assume that this banal source of evolutionary progress somehow devalues human life; that if chance errors have created humankind, we need not be taken too seriously. But that is not a logical conclusion to reach; it is one that assumes that facts determine values.

When human beings come to examine their own existence, they do so from a perspective that includes their subjective and active participation in the world. Issues about what one ought to do or the freedom of choice about one's future are a natural part of one's self-understanding.

There are two dangers here:

- We may fall into the 'naturalistic fallacy' trap, by attempting to make factual information the basis for social and moral imperatives. This is illogical, but understandable, since the personal aspects of life are broader in their application and may therefore be more relevant and important to us than the specific disciplines we use in scientific analysis of facts.
- By being concerned to look at the facts (in this case the successful mistakes that have led to the evolution of our species) and to avoid the naturalistic fallacy, we may be tempted to assume that personal or psychological features of life are in some way 'unreal' or irrelevant to science. That cannot be the case, since, as we shall see, they too are phenomena which can be the object of scientific investigation.

The status of social and psychological theories

In Chapter 7 of the *Origin of Species*, Darwin turns from his consideration of the physical properties of creatures to examine their instinctive patterns of behaviour. He argues that social activity, as he observed it in nature (e.g. in the ways ants work together, differentiating their functions within their community), could be accounted for using his general theory of natural selection. He argues that there is a 'slave-making instinct' that leads individuals within a colony to act in a way that enables personal goals to be set aside in favour of the goals of the colony as a whole.

Now it is clear (although Darwin did not take it to its logical conclusion) that humankind can be examined in exactly the same way. We see that society is organized in such a way that individuals sometimes need to sacrifice themselves for the good or the whole or, at the very least, they have to accept a particular role placed upon them by society.

Morality tends to follow from social differentiation, as we see when people feel instinctively guilty if they fail to do what is expected of them. Hence, much of what has been reserved for the personal, moral and religious aspects of life (and therefore previously largely untouched by the arguments and experimental methods of the physical sciences) can be seen in terms of the theory of natural selection.

This line of thinking has led to the development of sociobiology (see pages 132f), and its discussion about the degree to which our behaviour is genetically prompted in ways which reflect the basic genetic impulse to facilitate survival and breeding.

We find that, as science moves from a consideration of physical entities to look at the nature of humankind and society, we are likely to encounter a whole raft of problems, since the traditional 'two books' divide (with the personal or religious aspects of life on one side and the physical and scientific on the other) can no longer apply.

This aspect of Darwin's work therefore paves the way for a serious examination of humankind – in the disciplines of psychology and sociology. Is it realistic to take the step of applying his observations about ants and bees and apply them to human society?

We saw (page 23) that in the 19th century, as a result of the availability and analysis of statistics about human behaviour, sociologists and others started to examine human behaviour in scientific terms, looking for law-like patterns and regularities within, for example, the incidence of suicide in the population. As a result we see the development of studies of humankind that claim to be scientific, in that they follow the basic approach of inductive inference which characterized scientific method.

Hence we have the development of political science, sociology and psychology – all of which examine aspects of human life that had not previously been within the remit of science. Now, clearly, philosophy is concerned with all these, since they raise a whole raft of issues. For our purposes here, we will keep strictly within issues already raised within the philosophy of science and examine the extent to which these new sciences of humankind can be said to be 'scientific', in the sense of keeping within the parameters of accepted scientific method. To do this, we will look at two of the best known exponents of such new thinking: Marx and Freud.

Marx (1818–1883)

Karl Marx conducted extensive historical research into the causes of social and political change. He observed that human survival depended on the supply of food and other goods and that the function of society was to organize the production and distribution of these. He therefore pictured society in terms of networks of relationships, based on the fulfilling of human need. He saw all other aspects of society as shaped by this economic infrastructure.

A scientist takes evidence and frames hypotheses in order to explain it, from the hypotheses come predictions and the confirmation or refutation of the hypothesis depends on whether those predictions are subsequently proved correct. In Chapter 2, we saw this process as basic to the scientific method.

Now Marx had a great deal of evidence for social change. What he sought was a suitable theory that would account for it. His analysis of change in society was based on the idea of a 'dialectic', a central feature of Hegel's philosophy. This involved a process in which one situation (a thesis) produces reaction (its antithesis) and the two are then resolved (in a synthesis). Marx took this theory and applied it to the relationships involved in the supply of society's material needs. His resulting 'dialectical materialism' saw change in terms of the conflict between social classes.

Presented in this way, Marx has clearly followed established scientific principles in presenting his dialectical materialism. He has his evidence and has framed his theory on the basis of it. The problem was that Marxism was not valid science, according to Karl Popper, since a Marxist would not accept that any evidence could count against the basic theory. Thus, if every event can be interpreted in terms of dialectical materialism, none can count against it and it therefore fails a basic requirement that every genuine scientific theory (according to Popper) should be theoretically capable of falsification.

Thus, if dialectical materialism is simply a theory of social change, it can be validated or refuted by its predictions. Political upheavals in the 20th century witnessed the power of Marxist ideology, followed by its rapid decline, since its key predictions (e.g. the collapse of capitalism) failed to be confirmed and the process of social and political change did not appear to follow the lines of class conflict in the way that Marxist theory predicted.

Freud (1856–1939)

After training in medicine, Freud worked as a hospital doctor, taking a particular interest in neuro-pathology. He then set up in private medical practice, dealing with nervous conditions, especially hysteria.

He developed psychoanalysis as a means of exploring the origins of such conditions. Through the analysis of dreams and by the free association of thoughts, a person could be led to articulate feelings that had been locked within the unconscious, but which Freud saw as the cause of bizarre behaviour or nervous conditions.

The key question here for the philosophy of science is whether or not psychoanalysis should count as valid science, on a par with other medical sciences.

One crucial point to keep in mind in evaluating the relevance of psychological theories to the philosophy of science is that the information provided by a person about the state of his or her mind, or the memories they describe, cannot be checked to see if it is true or false. Feelings or sensations cannot be observed directly, since they are not part of the physical world.

If someone gives an account of what he or she has experienced in childhood, one might try to question it on the grounds of its being inherently unlikely to be true, but it is very difficult to refute it. Even if it could be proved that a 'remembered' event could not possibly have taken place, that does not render the memory irrelevant – for the important thing is that, for the person undergoing analysis, the memory is significant, even if without foundation in fact.

With the physical sciences, it is of key importance the experimental evidence can be reproduced in order for its accuracy to be checked. No such checking process is possible in the case of the material that forms the basis of psychoanalysis. Introspection is a valuable tool in the hands of psychologists and philosophers, but it is far from infallible, and it always has to be taken on trust.

Thus, the situation with Freud is quite different from that of Marx with respect to evidence used. For Marx it is historical, although it is possible for his interpretation to be incorrect. For Freud, it is unique and uncheckable and it is therefore not possible to falsify the results of the analysis. It can also be argued that science requires repeatable and substantial evidence; this psychoanalysis, by its very nature, cannot provide.

Comment

Clearly, this section has merely touched briefly on the issues that need to be explored when considering Marxism or psychoanalysis from the standpoint of the philosophy of science. Both areas have generated a huge literature, some of which would be considered within either political philosophy or the philosophy of mind.

Cognitive science

From time to time, a branch of philosophy may develop into a largely autonomous area of science. We saw, for example, that in the 17th century, what had been termed 'natural philosophy' adopted a particular methodology and discipline and became the basis of modern natural science.

Something similar is happening in terms of the theory of knowledge and the philosophy of mind. Philosophers have always debated how we can know anything about the world and whether such knowledge comes from experience or is developed from innate ideas. Overall, the approach has been to reflect on what we know and try to ascertain how it can be justified.

There was a period from the 1920s to the 1960s when many philosophers considered that the mind could not be spoken of in empirical terms, and therefore one had to remain silent about it. This view was linked to the more general concern to use empirical evidence and the scientific approach as the sole criterion of meaning – a view promoted by the logical positivists.

Many behaviourists saw mental descriptions (e.g. that one was sad or happy) as simply covert ways of describing sets of physical characteristics; if mental events were not in the physical world, they could only take on verifiable meaning by being translated into physical characteristics in this way. In other words, to say that one feels happy 'means' that one is smiling; to be in pain, means that one is jumping up and down holding one's leg!

Then, in the late 1960s, all that started to change and there emerged a new approach to the mind, based on philosophy, psychology, linguistics and computer science. It was the attempt to approach the mind and human knowledge in a scientific way, through experiment and observation, rather than simply reflecting on concepts or through introspection.

This, of course, was rather forced on philosophy by developments in parallel disciplines. Psychology and pharmacology were showing how mental processes could be influenced both through therapies and through drugs. It made no sense to say that the mind, which was being changed by these things, was essentially unknowable. Linguistics was being established as a separate discipline, using scientific methods to examine the nature of communication. Computer science was also starting to emerge to the point at which it made sense to ask how computers could replicate those processes, like logic or language, that were traditionally seen as entirely non-physical, mental functions. The very question, 'Can you make a computer that thinks?' breaks through the strict divide between mental and physical.

Hence cognitive science was born, an interdisciplinary approach to the scientific examination of human thought and knowledge. Today it is not limited to understanding the actual process of knowing something (cognition), but links with biology to examine matters related to the functioning of the brain.

Scientific method is now being applied to an area of human experience which previously had been thought to be closed to it. From the standpoint of the philosophy of mind, we find that science and the scientific method is coming to unblock something of a cognitive impasse in the subject, allowing new approaches to be made in some of the traditional problems, such as how we know something, the relationship between mind and body and our knowledge of other minds.

9 COSMOLOGY

Understanding the nature of the universe as a whole has always been a central quest for both science and philosophy. As we saw in Chapter 1, the rise of modern science, with its emphasis on observation and experiment and its use of mathematics, promoted a new approach to astrology. As we look at the work of Copernicus, Galileo, Kepler, Newton and others, we see both the quest to understand the structure of the universe, but more specifically to discover the laws of physics which would account for the movement of bodies, both heavenly and terrestrial.

In cosmology, there are two interrelated sets of questions:

The first question

What is the structure of the universe? How did it originate? What is its future? How did it develop its present form? By what physical laws can we understand its workings?

Questions of this sort have led us from the Ptolemaic Earth-centred universe, through Copernicus to Newton and on to the modern image of the world expanding outwards for the last 15 billion years from a **spacetime singularity** at what is known as the 'Big Bang'. They are concerned with order, structure and the process of development.

The second question

What is the simplest, most basic and most general thing we can say about reality? What lies beneath the multiplicity of what we see?

Questions of this kind started when Thales speculated that the world was essentially composed of water and the atomists tried to find the basic building blocks of physical reality. They were implied within the world of Newtonian physics by the quest for ever more general and comprehensive laws of nature. Today the quest is for a single 'theory of everything' that might show how the basic fundamental forces of the universe (electromagnetic, gravitational, strong and weak nuclear) are related to one another.

In modern cosmology, these two sets of questions come together. The structure of the universe has been determined by the forces operating within it. If we understand the one, we will also understand the other.

The personal angle

One of the issues that we have faced time and again within the philosophy of science is how to take into account the fact that what we observe is influenced by our own faculties of observation. Our understanding of the world is influenced by the way we examine it and the questions we consider it appropriate to ask of it.

This applies particularly to cosmology. In the Ptolemaic universe, it was considered that the heavenly bodies, on their glassy spheres, influenced events on Earth. Today, faced with the vastness and impersonal nature of the universe, there is a tendency to ask about significance and direction, about meaning and the place of humankind within the overall scheme of things.

These questions are philosophical and religious rather than scientific, but they can sometimes influence our interpretation of the evidence. A major issue here, which we shall examine later in this chapter is the 'anthropic principle', a principle which (in its strong form) attempts to argue from the fact of human existence to the structure of the universe required to bring it about.

Dimensions and structures

Our galaxy is spiral in shape and it rotates. It is thought to contain 100 billion stars and to be about 100,000 **light years** in diameter. The Sun is a smallish star, about 32,000 light years from the centre of the galaxy. It is estimated that there are at least ten billion galaxies. These are not spread evenly through space but are clustered.

Since it takes light a considerable time to travel from one part of the universe to another, we are looking back in time as we look out into space. If I observe a galaxy five million light years away, what I am actually observing is the state of that galaxy as it was five million years ago, when the light from it started its journey. From galaxies more than five billion light years away (which is still less than halfway across the known universe) that light started to travel towards me at a time before the Sun or planets of our solar system were formed. If an observer on that galaxy were looking in this direction today, he or she would see only dust clouds.

Dimensions

One of the staggering features of modern cosmology is the sheer scale of what is being detected. For example, in December 1997 a satellite detected a huge burst of gamma radiation. The burst lasted for only about a second, but it released as much energy as all the 10 billion trillion stars in the known universe put together. Originating in a very small area, probably no more than 100 miles in diameter, it must have involved conditions very like those of the first milliseconds after the Big Bang. Later, astronomers were able to focus on the area of space in the constellation of Ursa Major from which the burst had come and were able to detect its optical afterglow.

An event of that power is remarkable enough in itself. What is equally astounding, however, is the calculation that the event took place 12 billion years ago and that the light and radiation had taken all that time to reach Earth. To put that into perspective, the event took place somewhere around eight billion years before the Earth was formed.

The dimensions of the universe are equally astonishing in terms of emptiness. We tend to think that the Earth is solid and compact, but in reality it is, of course, mostly empty space, through which particles can pass unhindered.

This is illustrated by the findings, announced in June 1998, of a team of 100 scientists from 23 different institutions in America and Japan, following an experiment to detect and measure the mass of neutrinos, elementary particles so small that they are capable of passing through the Earth. Their work involved a tank of very pure water, one mile below the Earth's surface, in which, once every 90 minutes, a neutrino made its presence known by colliding with an oxygen atom and giving off a flash of blue light.

The project involved looking at the secondary particles that strike the Earth, following the bombardment of the upper atmosphere by fast moving particles from space. It is important for an understanding of the structure of the universe, because previously it had been thought that neutrinos had no mass. And this, of course, has important implications for the big issue of cosmology, namely whether the mass of the universe is such that its gravity will prevent it from expanding indefinitely (see page 158). Neutrinos may account for much of the missing or 'dark matter' that needs to exist to account for the apparent mass of the universe.

Comment

It is curious to think that the universe may take the form it has and have its future determined by particles so small that they can pass through the Earth undetected. It highlights the very narrow range of objects that human's generally regard as having significance. Visible matter is seen as significant simply because it is visible; other levels of material reality remain hidden, but are equally important

Einstein suggested that the universe could be seen as a hypersphere, and that one could move through indefinitely without ever reaching an edge, even if it were in fact finite, eventually coming back to the point from which one started.

This sounds bizarre, until one considers that general relativity showed that space and time are not fixed; space is bent in strong gravitational fields. But gravity is one of the fundamental forces that holds the universe together. Thus, all space is going to be bent to some very minute degree; and if space is bent, then it will eventually fold back on itself. The best way to envisage this infinite distance through a finite universe is in terms of moving round the inside surface of a sphere. You could turn any way you like and travel an infinite distance on that surface, but the surface itself remains finite. However far you travel, you will never be further away from any other point on that surface than the diameter of the sphere. (Ever watched a hamster on a wheel or in a ball?)

However, the theory proved to be a mistake. Einstein believed that such a universe could be finite and static. Why then did its gravity not cause it to collapse back in on itself? His answer was to propose the 'cosmological constant', representing a force that held things apart, frustrating gravity. Later, when it was shown that the universe was expanding and that the constant was therefore unnecessary, he admitted that it had been a blunder.

The 'Big Bang' theory

In terms of terrestrial experience, you can observe only the present, never the past. The past is, by definition, what no longer exists. In terms of the universe (because of the limitations imposed by the speed of light), the opposite is true. You cannot observe the present, only the past. The further you look, the further back you see.

There are, therefore, two basic ways of knowing about the past. One is to observe trends in the present (or, in cosmic terms, the very recent past) and trace them back into the past. At this moment, it can be observed that the galaxies are moving apart (both from us and from one another). The spectrum of light changes if the body being observed is moving away at very great speed. In 1929, E. P. Hubble observed a 'red shift' in the light coming from distant galaxies. Those galaxies that are furthest away from us are moving away faster than those nearer to us. Clearly, therefore, if the galaxies are moving apart, it follows that the universe is expanding.

From the speed of expansion, it is possible to calculate the age of the universe. Somewhere between ten and 20 billion years ago the present universe started expanding outwards in an 'explosion' known as the 'hot big bang' from a point where all space, time and matter were compressed into an infinitely small point, called a spacetime singularity. A crucial thing to appreciate about this theory is that a singularity is not a point within space and time, it is the point from which space and time have come. It is difficult to think of an explosion without thinking of matter flying outwards through space. But in this early stage, there was no space 'out there' through which matter could explode. Space is created as this expansion takes place. It is also confusing to say that the universe started from a point (a singularity) that was very small. Imagining a universe the size of a pea is confusing, because we automatically imagine a world outside that pea and yet (according to this theory) there is no 'outside'.

The process by which the universe takes its present structure is one in which energy becomes matter, spreading out uniformly in the form of hot gas. This then cools and condenses, gradually forming the galaxies.

However convincing this argument, it is still a projection of present trends back into the past. Yet the past is visible, if we look far enough. In theory, therefore, if the universe did expand out from this 'Big Bang', we should be able to look back through time and find some trace of it.

And the key to that, of course, is that – if space has 'grown' with the expansion – then the traces of the 'Big Bang' are not going to be located in any one place, but will be spread uniformly across the universe. Such direct evidence was provided in the 1960s, when background microwave radiation at 3° above absolute zero was found throughout the universe.

Every theory is confirmed or refuted on the basis of the things that it predicts – in other words, we have to ask what follows from it and then check out whether that is the case. In the case of the Big Bang theory, several quite obvious consequences have been checked:

- First of all, we can look for some evidence of that early state. That was found in the background radiation.
- Second, if the universe started as a Big Bang – in other words, in a state where everything was flying apart – then (unless gravity has proved strong enough to halt that expansion) it should still be expanding today. This has been confirmed by the observation of the 'red shift' in distant galaxies. The further away from us a galaxy is, the faster away from us it is moving. In other words, the universe is still moving apart.
- Third, if the universe expanded as predicted by this theory, there should be substantial quantities of the

light elements, particularly hydrogen, in the present universe. The quantities of these elements that are observed today are in line with the quantities predicted by the theory.

There are many outstanding problems here. One is to find out where the vast amount of matter and radiation in the present universe 'came from'. How is it that a sudden expansion of this sort comes about? Looking at the possible trigger for the Big Bang, the theory developed by Turok and Hawking sees its origins in what they term an 'instanton' – a point that includes space, time, matter and gravity. It lasts for no more than an instant, but has the ability to trigger the production of an infinite universe.

What is more, long before the galaxies were formed, we know that there was an unevenness in the universe, an unevenness that may have played a crucial role in determining how the hot gas condensed to form the sorts of structures we see today. Work over the last decade on the 'inflation' model, describes a state in which there is a very rapid expansion along with the spontaneous creation of matter and energy. This happens as the very first phase of the 'Big Bang'. Slight quantum variations in this inflationary stage might explain the later ripples of unevenness in the expanding universe, which in turn caused the formation of galaxies as the universe cooled.

Winding down or bouncing?

The Second Law of Thermodynamics describes the loss in terms of heat energy in every change of state. In other words: in any closed system, things gradually wind down. Applying this to the universe suggests that it should gradually dissipate its energy and end up in a state of total entropy (uniform disorder) having lost all its heat.

The outward momentum of the galaxies is countered, of course, by the gravitational pull exerted by their mass. A closed universe is one in which the expansion is slowing, due to the force of gravity and will eventually recollapse into itself. An open universe is one in which there is not enough matter to enable gravity to halt the expansion. Here there are all sorts of problems, well beyond the scope of this book, about the amount of matter in the universe and the theory that much of it is 'dark matter' which we cannot detect.

There is a possibility that, if its mass is large enough, and therefore gravity strong enough, we may reach a point at which the energy of expansion is balanced by the gravitational pull. From that moment of stillness, the universe would start to contract, eventually imploding into a 'big crunch'. One could then speculate that with such a violent compression of the universe into a singularity, there could be another 'Big Bang' with a new universe being formed. In other words, the universe could bounce!

Expanding space

The expansion of the universe is not 'through' space, but 'of' space. This is difficult to conceptualize, since – on the small scale seen on Earth – we see space as static; a metre rule remains one metre in length. Yet, if space is expanding, so is everything. The same process which propels distant galaxies away from us is also gradually pulling atoms apart and extending metre rules!

This book is therefore larger now than when you bought it – although this need not be cause for regret, since it will contain no more words! You cannot detect that expansion, however, since you and everything around you are also expanding at the same rate. It only becomes noticeable when observed over a distance of many light years.

Because the expansion of the universe is 'of' space rather than 'through' space, that expansion will appear the same from all points within space. In other words, there is no point in space from which this expansion is moving out – it is moving out from all points simultaneously. The 'Big Bang' did not happen somewhere else; you are part of its expansion.

Towards a theory of everything

Generally speaking, we have seen that science makes progress by examining a limited set of facts and working from them to formulate theories that may then be applied elsewhere. As theories come into contact with one another, they either clash (in which case the more productive and predictive tends to displace its rivals) or agree (in which case each is reinforced by the other). We have seen also that, as one general paradigm gets replaced by another, it is often because the earlier one was limited in its application. So, for example, Newtonian physics was shown to be fine, but only for the very limited conditions found on Earth, whereas Einstein's theories covered more extreme cases found elsewhere.

Logically, therefore, the process of refining and developing scientific theories is moving in the direction of a single theory capable of accounting for all phenomena everywhere: **TOE** – a 'theory of everything'.

In most cases, this is not a practical possibility. In examining living organisms, for example, we have seen that a reductionist approach (in which biology is reduced to chemistry, which in turn is reduced to the physics of the constituent atoms) does not do justice to the phenomenon as a whole. Additional theories are therefore required to show its operation on a holistic level. We have social theories about behaviour and medical theories about the operation of the body's various systems, which operate at a totally different level from those theories that describe the physics and chemistry involved. However, when we move into the field of cosmology, the possibility of a theory of everything becomes more realistic.

In the world as we experience it now, there are various forces and these operate over different dimensions. The nuclear forces are very powerful but operate over very short distances, holding atoms together. Gravity, by contrast, operates at a much weaker level, but over vast distances, holding objects onto the surface of the Earth or keeping the stars circling one another in galaxies.

Bump!

To test the relative strengths of the nuclear and gravitational forces, it is only necessary to fall over. Gravity will have the more obvious effect over a distance of about a metre or so, as you topple and fall. Contrariwise, at the moment of impact, the nuclear forces holding the atoms that constitute the ground and your body together are clearly superior over that very short distance and bring you to a sudden halt!

Indeed, it is just as well that the nuclear forces are stronger than gravity or you would end up as a puddle of sub-atomic particles!

The closer you get back to the singularity, the simpler the universe becomes. Once matter is formed from radiation and starts to move apart, the fundamental forces that are later to shape it differentiate from one another. Yet, at the point at which the whole universe is compressed into a single point, those forces cannot be separated. Just as, in the area of biological evolution, you may look back to a common ancestor for two related species, so in the area of fundamental physics, we may look for a common ancestor for all existing physical theories.

It is therefore, clearly, a quest for simplicity rather than complexity, reflecting the way in which the universe has moved from a very simple early state to the current more complex one.

Comment

The problem with describing a very small, compressed universe is that it is unimaginable. The most significant feature of a small-scale object is that its structure is simple, undifferentiated. Therefore, instead of imagining size, try to imagine structure.

Time and space are related to one another. Expansion can be imagined in terms of increasing differentiation: you see things stretching out, changing, cooling, taking on different forms, clumping together under the influence of gravity.

It might be easier to conceive of a very simple early universe, gradually becoming more complex or an extremely hot, uniform universe becoming gradually cooler and more differentiated.

The human perspective

The study of cosmology generally raises issues that go beyond the search for a mathematical theory to explain the origin and development of the universe. It does not remain simply a quest for information, but inevitably raises questions about the meaning and value of human life. The natural thing to want to ask about any general theory of the universe is where and how human life fits into it and whether it can have any lasting significance. Of course, the danger here from a scientific point of view is that these questions have existential and religious significance and it is therefore very difficult to examine them with strict objectivity.

The anthropic principle

> Imagine a universe in which one or another of the fundamental constants of physics is altered by a few percent one way or the other. Man could never come into being in such a universe. That is the central point of the anthropic principle. According to this principle, a life-giving factor lies at the centre of the whole machinery and design of the world.
>
> (J. D. Barrow and J. A. Tipler, *The Anthropic Cosmological Principle*, O.U.P., 1986).

There are two versions of the anthropic principle.

The weak version

If any of the major constants of the universe were different, we would not be here, life would not have evolved. Our life is dependent on the world being exactly as it is.

The strong version

The universe contains within itself the potential for life and it was therefore impossible for human life not to have been created in this world.

Let us examine the logic of this argument. It would seem to be this:

- If the universe were different from the way it is, we would not be here.
- Everything that happens is determined causally.
- Once the initial parameters of the universe were set – presumably at the 'Big Bang' – then it became quite inevitable that life would evolve and therefore that we would end up contemplating the universe.

This raises a fundamental question. We know that the initial conditions must have been what they were in order for this kind of universe to develop and therefore for us to be here. But did the universe have to be like this?

Now, the strong version of the anthropic principle makes it sound as though there were an element of compulsion in the early conditions of the universe; in other words, that they had to be what they were and that the universe therefore had no option but to develop life on this particular planet.

Here we need to remind ourselves of the basic feature of scientific laws, namely that they are the summary of experience, expressed in the form of a general proposition. They are either accurate or inaccurate in describing the world as it is – they do not command the world. You cannot 'break' a law of nature. Laws of nature do not determine what shall happen, they summarize what has happened.

Taken in its strong sense, the anthropic principle seems to imply an element of compulsion, that the universe has a purpose or goal, which is to produce human life; that we are not an optional extra, but built into the system from the first. But this goes against the whole descriptive nature of scientific theories.

In its weak sense, the anthropic principle says, in effect, that everything depends on everything else and, that, if anything were different, everything would have to be different. In a different universe, we would not be here.

That is no more than was claimed by Leibniz, who saw the whole world as a mechanism in which a change in one place implied changes elsewhere.

In effect the weak version is saying no more than 'if the conditions had not been right for humankind to have appeared, then humankind would not have appeared'.

This gets us nowhere in terms of understanding the original conditions of the universe. It is therefore quite possible to examine cosmology without being tempted to be drawn into the strong version of the anthropic argument, and its weak form really says nothing other than the commonplace that everything is as it is because of everything else and that if the world were different then we might well not be here thinking about it!

The chance of us being here...

'We are part of the universe.' This banal statement has enormous implications for an overall view both of cosmology and science as a whole. From the time of Descartes through to modern discussions of the anthropic principle, there has been a danger of separating humankind off from nature, seeing the world as something 'out there' to be understood or as a process whose sole purpose is to produce thinking human beings.

Seeing human beings as somehow 'outside' the natural world and treating the latter as little more than a vehicle and life support system for their own benefit leads to a distortion that we see frequently in terms of our terrestrial environment and the impact that humankind has upon it.

Comment

If we see ourselves as part of the universe, we should neither expect it to be there for our benefit, nor look for some kind of occult cause for the human existence or human thought. Modern physics recognizes that we influence all that we observe and that we cannot speak of objects independent of our perception of them. It seems to make the world subjective. We now see that this is not the case; that subject and object are simply conventional ways of dividing up experience. At a deeper level they are one and the same.

One of the features of the cosmos that inclines people towards an acceptance of the anthropic principle, is the unlikely sequence of events that must have taken place in order for human (or any) life to evolve on Earth. Once we examine the facts, however, we come across the old problem (see Chapter 6) about chance and necessity. On the one hand, everything is extremely improbable, in that it depends on a huge number of other factors being the case; but, on the other, it seems quite understandable and almost inevitable.

Take the example of planet Earth. Life is sustained on this planet because conditions are just right and, in particular, because it is a wet planet, with much of its surface covered with water, taken up into the atmosphere and deposited again as rain. Without water, there would be no life as we know it. Looking at neighbouring planets we see that life could not be sustained and we realize that it is only because our planet is a certain distance from the Sun that water can exist in liquid form and everything that follows from that simple fact.

Looked at in a different perspective, water is very common and is likely to be in liquid form on any planet that is orbiting at roughly this distance from its star. Far from being a unique case, the Earth may be simply one of a huge number of wet planets, spread throughout the galaxies – each with oceans, clouds and rain. After all, the elements of which we are composed are those found everywhere – why should we assume that the Earth is so special?

Getting the atmosphere right

At one time is was generally believed that the early atmosphere on the Earth was composed of huge quantities of methane and ammonia – not compatible with the development of oxygen-needing forms of life – but it was argued that, if you take methane, ammonia and water, expose it to ultraviolet radiation and then pass electric arcs through it, molecules are produced that will eventually start moving in the direction of life. Those required conditions would have been found on Earth, since the Sun would have provided the ultraviolet light and thunderstorms would have given rise to frequent bolts of lightening.

A more likely scenario (e.g. as set out in the very accessible collection of articles *The Case of the Missing Neutrinos* by John Gribbin) is that the atmosphere was at one time largely composed of carbon dioxide, some of which was absorbed by the oceans, but as life started to develop in the waters, oxygen was produced as a byproduct and this then built up, creating the ozone layer. This cut out ultraviolet radiation from the Sun and enabled the further development of life on dry land, which would previously have been destroyed by the radiation.

In other words, the atmosphere goes through a process of change; it was not created at the same time as the Earth itself, ready for life forms to appear. There is a process and particular forms of life fit into that process at particular points. That gives a 'place' for humankind within the general order of things in the universe; it does not require us to conclude that the whole thing was somehow shaped for our benefit.

In a way, everything is both extremely unlikely and also quite inevitable. But it does not imply that the whole thing was organized for the sake of humankind, simply that had it not happened in that way – humankind would not be here at all and life would have taken some different route.

Getting chance into perspective

A useful exercise might be to make a list of all those things required in order for it to be possible for life to appear on planet Earth (e.g. size of planet, distance from star). Then, against each of these, rephrase the requirement in general terms (e.g. life could appear on any planet that has... or is...).

Given the list of requirements, life looks extremely improbable and you might be tempted to adopt a strong anthropic argument and claim that the universe was designed for the sake of humankind. Given the almost infinite number of planets that are circling all the stars in all the galaxies, you need to ask:

- Is our Earth likely to be the only planet that has each of these qualities?
- If other planets have these qualities, is it not likely that life will appear on them?

Hence, from an impossibly specific set of requirements and an almost infinite number of planets, you reach the logical conclusion that life is quite likely elsewhere, but that our chances of ever encountering it are effectively nil!

The issue of life on other planets therefore has no practical implications, but, of course, it does have important existential and religious implications, since it displaces humankind from the privileged position it had given to itself.

Forward to the past

Whatever else it reveals, astronomy is a science that is supreme at putting human concerns into perspective. Our Sun is already well through its life-cycle and one day it will expand, destroying the Earth in the process. Even that, however, is merely a temporary and parochial incident compared with the future of the galaxy.

Our own Milky Way and the Andromeda galaxy are approaching one another at 300,000 miles per hour. They will eventually collide, either head-on or grazing against one another. This will start to happen in approximately 5 billion years' time and the process will probably take several hundred million years, involving the birth of millions of new stars as huge molecular gas clouds are compressed between the galaxies. Eventually, a new composite galaxy will form and all that we now see of our own galaxy will be totally transformed. From a narrowly human perspective, the elements will have returned to where they were before life appeared on Earth.

Comment

Such is the nature and dimensions of the universe, of course, that long after the material that presently forms the Earth, solar system and galaxy has been recycled, it will be theoretically possible to view it – just as it is today – from some distant point in the universe. Indeed, if it were possible to view the Earth and simultaneously move away from it at the speed of light, time on Earth would appear to stop.

What is clear, however, is where we stand in this process. The first-generation stars were formed about ten billion years ago, fuelled by nuclear fusion, as quantities of hydrogen were turned into helium and other heavier atoms were formed. After star death in a supernova, the resulting matter was scattered deep into space, gradually gathering into clouds which condensed under gravity to form another generation of stars and planets, ours included.

Every atom in our bodies was formed out of hydrogen inside a first-generation star. Every bit of what we are now was there in that generation of stars – the only difference was that the atoms were not gathered up and arranged in quite their present order!

What is clear, therefore, is that we can only appreciate the elements on Earth (or the existence of Earth itself) in the context of the whole history of the universe. From the time when energy turned into matter and matter clumped together, fuelling heavier atomic structures, a process has been going on of which we are a part. This is not to say (the strong anthropic principle tends to suggest) that the whole process was there for our benefit, designed in order that we could be produced. Rather, it is to acknowledge that we are a very small and very temporary incident in the ongoing cosmic story.

A curious reflection

Some of the most dramatic and influential discoveries in the early days of modern science were in the area of astronomy – Copernicus and Galileo immediately spring to mind. People were concerned about the movement of the planets, however, because of astrology, the utterly non-scientific theory that the planets had a direct bearing on events on Earth. The phases of the Moon and the movements of the planets were portents, to be interpreted (or misinterpreted) in order to know the future of events on Earth.

Astronomy moved away from astrology and showed movements that were predicted by mathematical calculation and mechanical laws. There seemed to be no more connection between the movements in the heavens and events on Earth.

Now it is astronomy that once again challenges human self-understanding. We are not separable from the stars. Our matter is not independent of theirs. There are not two substances, one heavenly and the other earthly, but only one. The material of which the heavens are formed is exactly that of which we too are made. Matter itself is universal; we are part of a whole of which the moving planets too have their part to play.

The crucial difference, surely, is this: that in a pre-scientific era it was possible to see occult forces at work defining events in the heavens and on Earth. Now we see only the outworking of a process, at once wonderful and threatening. We look at the night sky and know that, in a very literal and physical sense, we are part of all this.

10 SCIENCE AND AUTHORITY

In Chapter 3, we considered some of the ways in which theories gain acceptance within the scientific community, what gives them authority and what determines which theories survive and which do not in the competitive world of scientific research.

We looked at the work of Popper on the one hand and Kuhn on the other, examining the way each of them saw the process by which theories and paradigms are accepted and then replaced. The key question was seen as: Do we reject a theory as soon as some piece of contrary evidence is found or do we maintain a theory, in spite of its limitations, until another is found that is clearly more widely applicable?

But how does the authority given to a widely accepted theory (such that it will be replaced only when a crisis is reached) relate to the authority of the scientific establishment which accepts it? Lakatos emphasized that theories are developed as part of ongoing research programmes and that a theory is only discarded (or should only be discarded) when a better one is found, one that predicts new facts, for example. But how, in practice, does that process work? Who determines whether the new theory is in fact better than the old? Kuhn argued (see page 77) that it came about as a result of the overall view of the scientific community, taking a variety of factors into consideration. Clearly, the authority of a theory therefore depends on the consensus among and authority of the scientific community that maintains it as a working basis for ongoing research.

The expectation of authority

We also need to take account of the degree of authority that a 'scientific' claim is expected to have among the population at large, rather than simply within the scientific community. Sometimes the expectation that science will be able to give a definitive answer goes far beyond the reality of the more tentative claims that science actually makes. When a technical question arises in the course of a major health crisis – as, for example, on whether the combined MMR vaccine should be given to children, or whether mobile phones are dangerous if used for long periods – the public turns to scientists and expects them to provide definitive answers and practical solutions. This is not always possible and there is a danger that scientists will go along with the public's perception of their infallibility, simply in order to give an acceptable or reassuring answer:

> The sceptical public is unable to understand or unwilling to accept the nuances of probability involved in any scientific calculation and, aware of this, even the most well-meaning scientists are lured into claiming a degree of certainty which in their hearts they know is impossible.
>
> The reality of science is that, for all its startling achievements, it remains a tentative series of guesses about the nature of reality.
>
> (Bryan Appleyard, *Sunday Times*, 28 January 2001)

It may be misleading to take a quotation of this sort out of context. Appleyard does not argue that one person's guess at reality is as good as any other's. The point he is making is surely one that is totally in line with the majority of those who write on the philosophy of science; namely, that science is constantly looking for the best explanation that fits the evidence available. As observation and experimental evidence improve, so the conclusions to be drawn from them may change. A statement that is not open to revision is not scientific.

Perhaps one might therefore claim that most people do not want scientific explanations or advice at all; they want authoritative statements about reality. They want to know for certain whether something is or is not the case. They want to be told what they should do in order to keep well or save the planet. They want science to provide answers which are both correct and explicable in ordinary language. In other words: in turning to scientists for answers, both politicians and the general public often want the impossible.

In many spheres of life, the more authoritative a statement, the more likely it is to be true. If that is the case, then no scientific statement can claim absolute authority. To call a statement 'scientific' simply refers to the method by which the theory, on which the statement is based, has been brought about. The claim to be 'scientific' is not, in itself, a claim about truth; it may be true, in the sense that it is the best available explanation for the given evidence, but that is another matter.

Peer reviewing

In terms of the relationship between an individual scientist and the wider scientific community, one of the key factors in the acceptance of any theory is its publication in international journals, and its subsequent reviewing and testing by the scientific peer group. If an experiment cannot be repeated, or the same results are not obtained elsewhere, then the theory developed on the basis of that experiment becomes immediately suspect.

EXAMPLE

In 1989, two physicists, Martin Fleischmann and Stanley Pons, claimed that they had produced cold nuclear fusion. This was the attempt to create what would, if it worked, amount to a method of generating a theoretically infinite supply of energy, by harnessing the energy released in nuclear fusion. (Nuclear fusion can normally only be created artificially in the very energy-intensive conditions and, in these circumstances, the energy generated is far, far less than the energy used in the experiment. In nature, it is the process that keeps stars burning.) After extensive investigations their work was severely criticized. The problem was that other people failed to get significant results from their attempts to reproduce their experiment. That does not necessarily mean that they were wrong or that the goal of achieving cold nuclear fusion is not worthwhile, simply that they had not made the case for it in a way that would be acceptable to the global scientific community.

They were criticized not just on the grounds that the results of their experiment could not be confirmed, but because they had been secretive about their research, fearing that others might beat them to what was seen as a prestigious and lucrative discovery.

However 'objective' scientists claim to be, and however carefully the peer group examines theories put out by those who seem to deviate from the norm, it is clear that there are times when a scientist or group of scientists feels a commitment to a particular theory or research programme.

Whether it is a 'paradigm' (Kuhn) or a 'research programme' (Lakatos), there may be a sense that what is being explored – however much at odds with the findings of the rest of the scientific community – is too important to be discarded. Thus individual scientists are sometimes prepared to go against a widely held view, confident that in due course their own one will be validated. There are many examples of scientists who have been shunned for their individual views.

EXAMPLE

Linus Pauling, who was awarded a Nobel Prize for Chemistry in 1954 and had a prestigious career, was later regarded as extremely suspect for his view that vitamin C was a cure for many conditions and capable of extending one's life span. His commitment to that view set him at odds with the scientific community. Furthermore, that was not his only commitment, in that he was deeply involved with the protest movement against nuclear weapons. The achievements of an individual scientist do not, therefore, guarantee future acceptance of his or her views.

Sometimes, of course, a theory can be ridiculed at one time, only to be proved correct later. In 1912, Alfred Wegener was unsuccessful in arguing for his theory of continental drift!

In general, therefore, one may say that the scientific community tends to be quite conservative. Following the approach described by Kuhn and Lakatos, it is clear that it takes more than a single experiment to shift a widely held theory. Only when there is cumulative evidence of an inadequacy is a paradigm or research programme finally abandoned and replaced by another.

To some extent this is justified on any pragmatic or functional view of scientific theories – if a set of theories, or paradigms, is working well and yielding results, there is a tendency to keep to it until it finally gives way to another which clearly offers greater explanatory power. To the innovative thinker, this smacks of authoritarian conservatism. To the scientific community as a whole, it may be the safeguard against rash abandonment of all theories once they are challenged, with the possible failure to explore their full explanatory potential.

The social function of science

Scientific method aims to guard against the complaint that the findings of science are made to conform to the expectations of those who pay for it. It aims at objectivity, although, as will be clear by now, that is a very difficult thing to claim. At least, it is argued that science follows a methodology based on reason and evidence, rather than on political or economic expediency.

From time to time a scientific theory may be put forward, based on experimental evidence, which appears to go against what is regarded as politically correct. One example of this is Hans Eysenck who, through the 1960s and 1970s, did major work on intelligence testing. He came to the conclusion that there were differences in IQ related to differences in race. This led to the accusation of 'racism', implying that his findings reflected a moral and political bias. Clearly, what is at stake here is the authority of the scientific method: a scientist cannot claim as scientific any theory which has been produced to fit a required ideology, even if a certain amount of evidence has been discovered to support it. Rather, the theory needs to be the best available interpretation of the available data.

There is also the issue of money. Much scientific research is paid for by industry and is conducted within defined guidelines in order to contribute knowledge that will have commercial implications. Scientists have to earn a living and therefore have to undertake work that is able to attract sponsorship or some sort of funding.

Science, however fundamental, is seldom 'pure' in the sense that it is conducted simply for the sake of increasing the sum of human knowledge. Science and technology generally go hand in hand, with science providing the deep theoretical work upon which technology can be built.

Such commercial funding is not necessarily crude in its influence; it does not try to determine the results of research programmes. However, the very fact that funding is provided for those research programmes deemed worthwhile, actually defines and shapes the world of research. Research which may be interesting and worthwhile, but which does not seem to be leading to any area of profitable technology, may never attract funding and therefore may never get done.

Those who engage in weapons research funded by the government or research into food additives, paid for by a company that produces them, or into the environmental impact of various technologies are all working to an agenda. They have been set tasks. They seek to find evidence that will be of value to those who employ them. Their work in science is driven by economic, social or political questions.

EXAMPLE

At the time of the 'cold war' between the USSR and the USA, it was the Soviets who first succeeded in putting a satellite into orbit (*Sputnik*) and then sending a man into space (Yuri Gagarin). The response to this on the part of the US government was to increase the funding for space exploration. This was partly for military reasons, partly also in order to show that the USA was unrivalled in the world of science. When President Kennedy announced the plan to land a man on the Moon before the end of the 1960s, it was a declaration of national self-confidence or great political significance.

Vast amounts of resources were thrown into the development of nuclear weaponry, missile technology and guidance systems, from the 1950s, as well as the NASA space exploration programme. Hence the 'space race' was not so much a scientific as a political phenomenon.

Today, most of the hardware that is put into orbit is there to make a profit – mainly in the shape of communications satellites. This is not to deny that the early space programme yielded much valuable information, but simply to point out that the information gained by such research programmes and technologies was of secondary consideration when it came to funding. The pressure to succeed was political.

A valid case can be made for saying that governments should fund fundamental research, because it is from this that new ideas are born that might subsequently lead to highly profitable technologies. In this way, research can be presented as a long-term investment, with the fear that, if it is neglected, the result will be that a nation gradually slips behind in terms of science and technology and therefore in terms of the potential benefits, both to its own citizens and to exports that new technologies can bring.

In this sense, science is always socially determined. There may be a huge number of phenomena worth exploring, but only those that have some social use will be funded. Hence, even if the results of a research programme are not directly influenced by social pressures, the selection and operation of that same research programme may well be.

This applies also to the interpretation of scientific evidence. So, for example, experts in a particular field may be called on to comment on whether a particular food is safe, or whether the prolonged use of mobile phones by young people can pose any threat to their health. As we saw earlier, there is a general expectation on the part of the public that scientists will provide definitive answers – how then (in practical terms) does the scientist face the media knowing that he cannot provide the sort of answers that are required?

Here there is a real problem in terms of the clash between scientific method and the public use of scientific information. Almost every activity involves some sort of risk, but in most cases the risk in minimal and is therefore ignored. Nevertheless, in a world where people might sue for negligence, it is essential to get some professional judgement about what constitutes 'danger to health' or what is an 'acceptable risk'.

What is clear is that all science can be expected to provide is the evidence – suitably explained – on which a judgement can be made.

It may set out the results of a series of carefully controlled tests; it may have gathered statistics from the population as a whole; it may present a host of facts and figures. What it cannot decide is what constitutes 'acceptable risk': that is a political or moral question, not a scientific one.

Note

This has many practical consequences – for example the calling of 'expert witnesses' in a court of law or the assessment of scientific evidence by government bodies responsible for safety legislation and the like. Just because an individual is a professional scientist, does that mean that his or her word should be taken as the final one on a matter that can have important social consequences?

Consider these instances:

- Scientific evidence was given in the original assessment of the BSE outbreak in British beef cattle and the balance of the assessment suggested to the government of the day that there was no need to be alarmist about the eating of British beef. Only later was the scale of the problem with variant CJD (the human equivalent of the 'mad cow disease') brought to light.
- Various scientists offer advice on the safety of using mobile phones – but there is no overall agreement on the scale of risk that they involve. Should a scientist be held liable for damage caused as a result of a failure to give a definitive warning about dangers? Or, equally, should the publication of the best available scientific evidence be a sufficient defence on the part of a phone company if they are sued by someone claiming to have been harmed?
- Government health warnings are printed on packets of cigarettes, based on best scientific evidence of the relationship between smoking and various diseases. Should that imply that the government need have no legal responsibility to support those who are made ill through going against its 'scientific' advice?

These are just a few of the many examples where people expect science to contribute to debates which have important political, legal, social or environmental implications.

In ethics, the philosopher G.E. Moore pointed out that, you cannot derive an 'ought' from an 'is' – a well-known error that he called the 'naturalistic fallacy'. Exactly the same fallacy applies to an attempt to define what is 'acceptable risk' or 'harmful' or 'beneficial' solely on the basis of scientific research. Qualitative judgements of this sort can only be validated with reference to the norms and values of society.

The threat of science and technology

The 17th and 18th centuries, during which science and technology developed and established themselves as a significant force in Western culture, were a time of some optimism. On the political as well as the scientific front there was a sense that humankind should make progress, based on reason. Research and experiment were features of science that fitted well with the overall view of life. The 19th century saw great developments in technology, as well as the great controversies between science and traditional religious authority, particularly over evolution. The groundwork for much 20th-century science was done in the latter part of the 19th century.

Nevertheless, science and technology did not develop totally unopposed during this period. The Romantic Movement of the 19th century may be seen against the background of a world newly mechanized and appearing to be increasingly dominated by science and technology. Artists, poets and philosophers could make a case for a world in which human emotions and Locke's secondary sensory qualities took precedence over the theories of science and mathematics.

EXAMPLE

Blake wasn't too happy about the technology that had sprung from the new science and he was deeply opposed to the rationalism of Locke and Newton, wishing to replace it with something more imaginative and intuitive. His image of Newton is of the oppressor who measures the Earth with a pair of dividers. Hence also the 'dark, satanic mills' that disfigured the countryside in which he seeks to build *Jerusalem* in his famous poem.

It was not merely the artistic temperament that railed against the increasing imposition of science and technology. From the standpoint of existential philosophy – with its emphasis on the meaning and purpose in human life – Sören Kierkegaard considered that science was quite capable of describing inanimate objects, plants and animals. 'But to handle the spirit of man in such a fashion is blasphemy' (from his *Journals*, quoted by Passmore, see page 179).

In many ways, the early years of the 20th century, both in philosophy and in science, were times when progress was seen as inevitable. Science and reason had prevailed over superstition, technology had given great benefits and all was set fair for a new world of reason and human triumph.

Then came the traumas of the 20th century, in war, in political instability and global rivalry between conflicting ideologies, in the loss of certainty (in science, as much as in life in general). The science and technology whose benefits had remained largely unchallenged, started to be questioned. The science that offered endless cheap fuel was also capable of nuclear holocaust on a global scale. Medical technology made huge strides in countering disease, yet the demands made upon it increased faster than it could deliver. Life-saving technology was not simply marvelled at, it was demanded. A medical answer was expected for every condition. Medical and nursing ethics were born as a philosophical discipline, largely in order to cope with the human issues raised by the availability of new technology.

In the 1960s and 1970s, many were critical of science. The promise of a better life through technology, championed in the post-war years, appeared to many to have a downside in terms of the threat of global extinction through nuclear war, pollution of the environment and gross inequalities fuelled by technologies and consumerism. Science was sometimes portrayed as narrow, as conducted by myopic men in white coats. It contrasted with the rising tide of self-expression, anti-war demonstrations and the hippie culture. A fascinating book from this era, looking at the criticisms lodged against science, is John Passmore's *Science and its Critics* (Duckworth, 1978).

The technology that was capable of increasing crop yields through pesticides was challenged for poisoning the environment. Mechanical devices that could increase agriculture and fell forests, yielding profits from those who could now look beyond their own area was seen as threatening a global natural resource, as rainforests diminished. The wonders of the modern aerosol and internal combustion engine were criticized for depleting the ozone layer and contributing to global warming. Global communication and information technology created wonders and also induced stress. A generation of obese children sat in front of television sets and played computer games.

Today, much of the criticism of science comes from those who fear that the technologies it makes possible will be imposed upon the world with inadequate appreciation of their impact. In this, science is often lumped together with big business.

Note

Against this, one may set the debate about biodiversity. Scientists have shown the value, both in environmental terms and also as a resource for future research, in maintaining the range of species presently on Earth. They have also shown the implications of destruction of environments on global ecological systems. In this, the consensus of the scientific community seems to be at odds with the generally exploitative and shorter-term views of business. Thus, even though there are cases where the science is funded by, and may therefore tend to justify, the economic exploitation of technology, it would be quite incorrect to generalize on the relationship between business and the scientific community as a whole.

Over a period of time, different branches of science are seen as a particular threat. Thus, in the 1960s and 1970s it was nuclear physics, with the threat of the arms race and its threat of nuclear holocaust. By the 1990s, with the changed political situation, the threat was focused more on the impact of technology on the environment (e.g. threats posed by genetically modified crops) and on the treatment of other species, especially the use of animals in scientific research.

Although criticism is generally levelled at particular applications of technology, there also appears to be an underlying fear that the very success of science will enable it to set its own agenda.

EXAMPLE

Cloning a human being is not an unrealistic scientific project. It may well provide additional technologies in terms of treatment for infertility. It may give single people the 'right' to have a child without the need for the direct or indirect input of a partner. It might be possible to produce hybrid creatures with many human features, produced in order to be used for transplants, for example, or as suitable subjects for medical experimentation. But the ethical question is this: just because cloning is possible and just because it might yield results of general benefit, does that make it right? Should the scientific community be able to explore anything, just because it is possible?

GM crops are another contentious area. There may indeed be benefits from genetically modified crops, but – even if these could be shown to outweigh the potential harm that such crops could do to the environment – does that automatically give scientists the right to trial and produce them?

Some people answer such dilemmas from a **utilitarian** standpoint. In other words, if the benefits outweigh the actual or potential damage, one should go ahead and do it. But one of the classic problems with utilitarianism is that it is never possible to get a final evaluation of gains and losses – a short-term gain may lead to a severe long-term loss, we may have no means of knowing. Hence, some people argue from a more absolutist viewpoint – about either human nature, or the purpose of human life – in order to evaluate whether a particular scientific activity should be allowed.

Comment

Science and technology deal with Aristotle's 'efficient' causes, not his 'final' causes. In other words, they deal with means, not ends. Those arguing from an environmental standpoint are generally dealing with 'ends'; namely, the quality of life that human beings can enjoy.

If you consider an object or event to be adequately and exhaustively defined in terms of its material and efficient causes, you are unlikely to have many reservations about the scope of scientific enquiry. If a human hybrid is 'grown' for medical purposes, it has no meaning, purpose of design over and above the technology that brought it about. One may therefore choose to use it on purely utilitarian grounds.

By the same token, if there are areas of life which you feel are not adequately or exhaustively described in terms of material and efficient causation, you are likely to take a stand in terms of whether something 'ought' to be done, basing your views on criteria that are not themselves the product of the scientific process.

In other words, you will be challenging the autonomy of science from the standpoint of 'metaphysics'. This has sometimes been treated as a pejorative term – as a dogma or belief that is out of touch with reality. It need not be so, however. It is simply a way of dealing with those areas of meaning and purpose which are included in human thought and language, but which are not themselves the straightforward product of evidence or sense experience.

EXAMPLE

One of the most intensely debated issues in recent years, in terms of science and the environment, has been that over genetically modified crops. Multinational companies such as Monsanto argued that the benefits to be gained from genetically modified crops (resistance to disease, increased yields) outweighed the largely unknown threat to the environment from the arrival of modified strains of otherwise natural plant species. Environmental arguments could be made for both sides of the debate, with the threat to other species of genetically modified crops, on the one hand, and the promise that such crops would do away with the need for ecologically more damaging fertilizers and would yield better produce both in terms of quantity and quality, on the other.

Interestingly, a biologist such as Edward Wilson (who developed sociobiology) is deeply committed to enhancing the environment, particularly in terms of maintaining biodiversity and yet feels – within that overall aim – an important part may be played by genetically modified species.

Often, the issue is not simply one of science versus the environment, or one of scientist versus non-scientist, but of the degree of freedom that should be allowed to commercial companies, whose use of science is geared to its fundamental business of making a profit.

In other words, the fear is that science and technology are likely to be pushed for reasons other than an altruistic desire for knowledge and general human benefit. Whereas the early scientists took the view that humanity could not fail to benefit from the triumph of reason, modern scientists have a more complex pattern of motivation and funding to cope with. Criticism of science is often aimed primarily at the process of control and monitoring (or lack of it) that is needed to ensure that there is overall benefit to be gained from a particular line of research or new technology.

In short, while science made huge strides in the 20th century, it also met with some major challenges in terms of justifying itself within the whole human project. Science had become a beast that needed to be controlled. Life was unthinkable without it, but at the same time, unfettered science and technology were seen by many as threatening the very quality of life that they aimed to enhance.

POSTSCRIPT: THE QUEST FOR KNOWLEDGE AND CONTROL

The word 'quest' may seem a strange one to introduce into a book on the philosophy of science, since is has overtones of the mystical or the romantic. It does, however, cover two important areas – the sense of purpose and direction and the sense of identity. A quest is a process which looks to some end product. One can therefore speak of the 'scientific quest' in terms of the long-term goals and overall rationale of science.

It is clear that many of those who laid the foundations of modern science were optimistic about the benefits to be gained from the application of human reason. Within the broad movement that we call the Renaissance, men and women were of the view that reason would replace crude superstition, that life could and should be examined and that the world could be understood in a way that would allow humankind a more positive measure of control over its destiny. This very positive of the goal of natural philosophy is found in thinkers such as Francis Bacon and Descartes. Indeed, Descartes made it clear in his *Discourse on Method* (1637) that he was deliberately moving away from speculative philosophy towards a practical philosophy that would aid humankind through the control of nature.

With the expansion of scientific knowledge in the 18th century, science emerged from under the umbrella of 'natural philosophy'. Philosophy was increasingly concerned with discussions about the theory of knowledge, rather than with practical experimentation. Science was starting to impact on a wider public through the development of new instruments and technologies, leading into the Industrial Revolution and the many changes to life that it brought. The impact of science was twofold: it offered both knowledge and control.

Some have seen the function of the philosophy of science as limited to an exploration of the methods by which science operates, the language it uses and the way in which it justifies its claims. That is, of course, a perfectly valid function, but it leaves out several crucial questions. Just as one cannot imagine studying ethics without taking into account the impact on society of the actual moral choices that people make, so it seems inadequate to have a philosophy of science that does not also address the impact that its knowledge and (through technology) its control over nature has had.

And, of course, the human world has been profoundly changed by the developments of science and technology. Few today would wish to reject all the benefits of modern medicine, communication or travel. In this sense, it is difficult to argue with the claim that science has been humankind's biggest success. Species in general have survived by adapting to fit their environment; humankind has gone a long way to adapting its environment to suit its own survival.

Ways of seeing ...

The process of science is one of abstraction, of framing principles that enable predictions to be made. The phenomena considered by science are therefore quite different from the sensual experiences enjoyed by human beings. It analyses and tabulates, searches for causal connections and makes predictions. If human experience is multicoloured, then some have seen in science the tendency to reduce everything to a mathematical grey. This was the complaint of Romantics like Blake and is implied by modern complaints about the 'reductionism' of science.

A key thing to remember here is that science does not (or should not) claim to be the only way of experiencing life. A knowledge of optics does not replace the act of seeing, but (through spectacles, or other instruments) may enhance it. Similarly, the human genome may reveal that 30,000 pieces of information, spelt out in letters formed of the four chemical bases on DNA, are sufficient to enable a human being to be put together. But that does not destroy the wonder of human life.

Science may show that we are very closely related to chimpanzees, but is that a negative statement or a positive one? That is surely not to denigrate human beings, but to celebrate what a difference a small genetic change can make.

Ordinarily when an event occurs, or when we encounter something, that thing or that event is the result of an infinite number of particular causes that have brought it about. The stranger I meet is uniquely the result of a sequence of childbirths through the generations that have produced this person with a distinctive character and a distinctive genetic profile.

In other words, everything we encounter is, in some respects, unique. But if something is unique, it is unrepeatable. And if it is unrepeatable, then we cannot use it as the basis to predict any future happenings. It is just there and there is nothing more to say.

Now, science cannot work on the basis of the absolute uniqueness of events. It works by abstracting general theories that can subsequently be applied to a range of events. The world can become predictable because, whenever we come across something, we understand it in terms of general terms and ideas that we have built up through our experience.

EXAMPLE

I see a tree. But I do not just stare at this large thing in front of me (although I might, if I am a very young child). Rather, I start to say 'it is a tree', 'it is an oak'; 'its leaves are fresh and brightly green because it is spring'; 'it gathers nutrients from the soil by drawing up water'. I am relating this particular experience of a tree to general features and it is these that constitute the knowledge of science. Science can show me how this thing grows and why I see it as having certain colours. It can talk about the effect of sunlight on chlorophyll and the way in which sap is drawn up the trunk. It can measure the oxygen exhaled and the carbon absorbed. What it cannot do is replace the *experience* of the tree.

We therefore need to remember that science is one but *only* one of the ways of encountering and understanding reality. If I am to fall in love, have a religious experience, act morally or produce something creative in the arts, I may need skills quite other than those of reason and analysis. Looking, responding, ascribing value: these are human ways of relating to the world that are non-scientific.

Science is therefore a valuable but *limited* way of encountering the world. In reality it has never claimed to be anything else. There are other ways of seeing.

However, this is far from saying that science presents a mundane, factual, unexciting view of the world, when we contrast it with the sense of awe generated by the arts or by religion. In *Unweaving the Rainbow* (Penguin, 1998), Richard Dawkins argues that the amazing features of our world, revealed by science, serve only to promote a sense of awe and wonder at nature. He shows that there is something amazing in the fact that we are alive at all, that the Earth provides exactly what is needed for human life to have evolved. A brief reflection shows that so many things have had to have happened in the past for us to have been conceived and born in this time and place. A minor chance occurrence to one of our ancestors and we would not exist in the way we do. In a sense, he shows how fragile and unlikely our life is, but also how wonderful. Facing the facts about how the most beautiful things have come about – unweaving the rainbow, and seeking to understand the science of light's different wavelengths – is not to decrease their power to induce wonder, but to enhance it. He regards the whole effort to understand the world in which we live for such a brief time as in itself a noble quest.

Ways of controlling ...

Seeking practical answers to problems is not new. The earliest known stone tool, found in East Africa, dates from about 2.6 million years BCE. The most important inventions for the survival and development of the human species were made a long time ago: fire; weapons for hunting and self-preservation; shelters; boats; the cultivation of crops; pottery; the weaving of cloth; the domestication of animals. By 3,500 BCE the arrival of the wheel opened up a whole new range of activity, and heavy weights were transported using rollers. Even in the 21st century we marvel at the ability of our ancestors to move the huge stones that make up the Pyramids or Stonehenge. By the second millennium BCE chariots with spoked wheels gave some peoples and cultures (e.g. the Aryans who invaded north-west India) an advantage over others.

None of this is science in the way we think of it, however. It does not involve the systematic putting forward of hypotheses and testing them out with carefully planned experiments, but a moment's reflection will reveal that the fundamental process – looking at problems and thinking about possibilities for overcoming them – are the same. Early man observes that friction produces heat and moves from that to discover that rubbing sticks together can produce a flame. No doubt there was a great deal of trial and error in the process, but the process was one of needing to know and of finding ways of achieving what was wanted.

Science offers a positive heuristic; in other words it seeks to find answers to problems, largely on the basis of trial and error, in an ongoing programme of research. In this, it is fuelled both by the need to create practical technologies to solve various human problems, but also to satisfy human curiosity and the need to ask fundamental questions.

As an example of the first, we have research into the basis of cell division and replication, which leads to an appreciation of how cancer cells develop and multiply, with a view to creating an effective treatment for that disease. As an example of the second, there is the fascination with the origins and structure of the universe or what happens as matter approaches a 'black hole'. There is no immediate practical technology to be derived from this, but it is human to want to know how the universe works.

In looking at the philosophy of science, we tend to think that pure science, the desire to know, freed from the need to show practical use, is fundamental and that technology comes along afterwards, bringing with it both benefits and threats. In fact, that process has been a very recent one – and it is only the availability of a leisured class (in Ancient Greece or 18th-century England) able to spend time in general speculation, that has produce the phenomenon of pure science or pure philosophy – for most of the time that human beings have been thinking and creating, their work has been in response to need. It has been demand led; and it has justified itself by its results. Medical science does not develop in a completely healthy world!

We have already noted that where funding for science is given for commercial reasons and new technologies are quickly developed and exploited, the way in which scientific research programmes are evaluated is likely to be quite different from the days when scientists were gentlemen of leisure, unaffected in their deliberations by the necessities of trade or the approval of the populus.

A broad-based philosophy of science needs to recognize and monitor what we may call the social or participatory aspects of science, for science has developed in response to human inquisitiveness and human need and its impetus is the need to solve problems. Science does not and cannot answer all human questions. In particular, as we saw earlier, it cannot provide a value-based justification for its own activity. Thus, it may be technically possible to separate Siamese twins, in the hope that one will be able to survive, but the issue is then raised as to whether this is the 'right' thing to do. Medical science says what is possible; it is then left up to those concerned with the law and with ethics to decide whether what is possible should be made actual.

The astounding contribution, but also the threat, of modern science is that it has given humankind so many possibilities, which can be used for good or ill. Philosophy is the 'love of wisdom'. A philosophy of science – in the broadest sense – is clearly essential if humankind is to benefit from what science continues to achieve.

GLOSSARY

analytic statements – those whose truth is established by definition (e.g. logic and mathematical statements), rather than by evidence (*see* **synthetic statements**)
atomism – the theory (first put forward in the 5th century BCE) that all matter is composed of atoms separated by empty space
correspondence theory – the theory that the meaning of a word is given by the object to which that word corresponds (problematic if we have no independent knowledge of objects)
determinism – the philosophical view that all things are totally conditions by antecedent causes
epicycle – the path traced by a point on the circumference of a circle as that circle is rolled around the circumference of a larger one; used for calculating the orbits of planets up to the 17th century.
final cause – the purpose of a thing; the actualization of its essence and potential (in Aristotelian philosophy)
holistic – describes an approach, argument or view that considers the operations of the whole of a complex entity (as opposed to its constituent parts)
induction (inductive inference) – the logical process by which a theory is devised on the basis of cumulative evidence
instrumentalism – the view that scientific laws are to be assessed by the results they yield
light year – the distance travelled by light in one year, at a speed of 186,000 miles per second
logical positivism – a school of philosophy from the first half of the 20th century, which, influenced by the success of science, attempted to equate the meaning of a statement with its method of verification

natural philosophy – the branch of philosophy which considers the physical world; a term used to include science prior to the 18th century

Occam's Razor – the principle that one should opt for the simplest explanation; generally summarized as 'causes should not be multiplied beyond necessity'

paradigm – a theory or complex of theories which together set the parameters of what is accepted as scientifically valid within its particular sphere of study, Kuhn describes how paradigms may eventually be replaced if they prove inadequate

phenomena – those things that are known through the senses; in Kant, it is the general term used for sense impressions, as opposed to **noumena**, or things as they are in themselves

primary qualities – a term used by Locke for those qualities thought to inhere in objects and are therefore independent of the faculties of the observer (e.g. shape)

reductionist – used of a process which analyses complex entities into their component parts and (by implication) ascribes reality primarily to the latter

scientism – the view that science gives the only valid interpretation of reality

secondary qualities – a term used by Locke for those qualities used in the description of an object that are determined by the sensory organs of the perceiver (e.g. colour)

spacetime singularity – a theoretical point of infinite density and no extension, from which the present universe, including space and time themselves, is thought to have evolved

synthetic statements – those whose truth depends upon evidence (*see* **analytic**)

TOE – a 'theory of everything'; the attempt to find a single theory to account for the four fundamental forces of nature (gravity, electromagnetic, strong and weak nuclear)

utilitarianism – theory by which an action is judged according to its expected results

Weltanschauung – term used for an overall view of the world, through which experience is interpreted

FURTHER READING

There are many substantial introductions to the philosophy of science for the serious student, and a huge number of books covering particular issues. Those listed here are no more than a personal selection.

For an anthology covering many of the key articles and central questions see: *Philosophy of Science: The Central Issues*, Martin Curd and J. A. Cover, Norton & Co, 1998.

For a very readable approach, try *What is this Thing called Science?* A. F. Chalmers, Open University Press, 3rd edn, 1999.

For the serious student, *The Philosophy of Science*, David Papineau (ed.), in the Oxford Readings in Philosophy series (OUP, 1996) is an important collection of key themes, which are readable although densely packed.

The *Philosophical Papers* of Imre Lakatos, published by Cambridge University Press in 1978, four years after his death, is a valuable collection of his work on the philosophy of science, summarizing some of the key debates of the mid-20th century with clarity. The first volume, *The Methodology of Scientific Research Programmes*, is particularly useful.

Particular areas within the philosophy of science are explored in readable fashion in the following:

For an historical and philosophical introduction to the issues of scientific method: *Scientific Method*, Barry Gower, Routledge, 1997.

For the philosophy of mind, especially artificial intelligence, see: *Minds, Brains and Computers*, R. Cummins and D. D. Cummins (eds.), Blackwell, 2000.

The Taming of Chance, Ian Hacking (CUP, 1990) looks at the way in which the gathering of statistics led social scientists to frame 'laws' that predicted outcomes without taking away the freedom of individuals to select how they should act.

For the whole issue of induction, *Fact, Fiction and Forecast*, Nelson Goodman, 4th edn (Harvard University Press, 1983) is the classic text, originally appearing in 1954 and much quoted.

For a modern account of evolution, try *Almost like a Whale* by Professor Steve Jones (Doubleday, 1999).

For a fascinating collection of articles on science (not strictly on the 'philosophy of science', but raising many issues and whetting the appetite to ask questions): *The Case of the Missing Neutrinos*, John Gribbin, Penguin, 2000.

Covering far more issues than even the title would suggest: *The Collapse of Chaos: Discovering Simplicity in a Complex World*, Jack Cohen and Ian Stewart, Penguin, 2000.

Richard Dawkins' books provide a wonderfully readable overview of science. *The Blind Watchmaker* (1986) gives a fascinating account of evolution by natural selection. *Climbing Mount Improbable* (1996) shows how the complexity of life can be accounted for through the small incremental changes brought about by evolution. *Unweaving the Rainbow* (1998) shows how a scientific analysis, far from detracting from a sense of wonder, actually expands and deepens it (all available from Penguin).

Within Hodder & Stoughton's *Beginner's Guide* series, there are volumes offering brief introductions to the work of Einstein, Darwin and Newton.

For an examination of the personal and religious issues raised by science, see *Religion and Science* in Hodder & Stoughton's *Access to Philosophy* series.

There are journals specializing in the philosophy of science (see *The British Journal for the Philosophy of Science*). Articles may sometimes be tough going and assume a good background knowledge.

INDEX